MORE THAN A GAME

SPORT IN OUR TIME

SEBASTIAN COE

DAVID TEASDALE
DAVID WICKHAM

BBC BOOKS

For Nicky, Mary and Pam

BBC Books would like to thank the following for providing photographs, and for permission to reproduce copyright material. While every effort has been made to trace and acknowledge all copyright holders, we would like to apologise should there have been any omissions.

L = left, R = right

A.F.L. (American Football League) Hall of Fame page 24; Allsport/Simon Bruty 6 10, Dave Cannon 19L 190/191, Steve Powell 28 34/35 96 & 235, Bob Martin 33 163, Stephen Wade 50L, Rettalita 50 R, Tony Duffy 55 59 & 94/95, Mike Powell 65, Gary Mortimer 69 72 & 90, Pascal Rondeau 100 168/169 206 208/209 210/211 213 216 217 & 234, Barey/Vandystadt 103, Vandystadt 104/105 110, Don Morley 113 120 & 147, Billy Stickland 150/151, Chris Cole 170, Chappaz/Vandystadt 181, Caryn Levy 187, Adrian Murrell 188; Associated Press 11 16 66 L&R 116 122/123 125 193 & 225; Barcelona Olympics Committee 227 (montage: Allsport/Pascal Rondeau, Jay Daniel, NASA); BBC/Chris Lanning 3 37 & 40; Bob Thomas Sports Photography 78 80/81; Brylcreem 183; M. Carlucci 74/75; Golf World 230; Hulton Picture Company 16 19R 22/23 36 52/53 58/59 136 & 156; Hutchison Library/Ann Tully 14; source The Independent 179; International Herald Tribune 102; Popperfoto 26 114 & 197; Quadrant Picture Library 106/107; Radio Times 155; Rex Features 228/229; RSPCA 92; Sports Illustrated (South Africa) 141; Syndication International 182 195; Colin Taylor 159; Tyrrell Racing/Zoom Photographic 98; UPI/Bettmann 231 L&R; Paul Zetter 25.

Picture Research by P. Alexander Goldberg and James Clift of Image Select. Special thanks to Daryl Ingham, Lee Martin, Tony Hicks and Joan Fisher.

Published by BBC Books,
a division of BBC Enterprises Limited,
Woodlands, 80 Wood Lane, London W12 0TT
First published 1992
© Sebastian Coe, David
Teasdale and David Wickham 1992
ISBN 0 563 36231 6
Set in Baskerville
Printed and bound in Great Britain by Butler & Tanner Ltd, Frome, Somerset
Colour separations by DOT Gradations Ltd, Chelmsford
Jacket printed by Lawrence Allen Ltd, Weston-super-Mare

Contents

Acknowledgements

It's always invidious to try to thank adequately everyone involved in a project of this kind. We have received a great deal of help and advice, from friends, families (particularly Sian Teasdale and Stefan Wickham) and old and present colleagues. Many are quoted in the text and we thank them for being so frank, relevant and interesting. Specifically, we must pay tribute to Jan Anderson, whose sharpness of mind and insight inform most of these chapters. The whole production team at Independent Image deserve mention for the efforts they have made while racing to put together the television series. The programmes' producers, Jonathan Jones, Greg Lanning, John Sheppard and Carrie Thomas, and researchers Sallyann Kleibel, Thelma Rumsey, Philip Wearne and particularly Mike Scott, have done a terrific job in meeting the book deadlines. We especially want to thank Anne Fitten Glenn for her tireless research and for co-ordinating all the chapter additions and amendments; and David Harrison, the series producer, for his gentle humour and perceptive questions and advice. To all these, and the many others who encouraged and assisted us at various times, attaches great credit; and no blame. We three alone are responsible for the mistakes here, whatever they are.

Sebastian Coe
David Teasdale
David Wickham

Preface

Sport spreads over a huge canvas. Its history, its place in society and its controversies bring dramatic colour to arguments and subtle tones to insight. No one book can hope to contain all the pictures in its gallery.

So we have been selective, and the following pages bear our prejudices and our passions. The foremost of these is that sport is a vital part of life and politics; and we have tried therefore to highlight those times and matters where sport has most touched our everyday lives, and most troubled our consciences. We three authors have come at it from different positions – the competitor, the administrator and the journalist. Each of us has worked in sport and with sport and sportspeople and seen 'action' at all levels. Sport for us is *More Than A Game*. We hope these pages will add a little to the pleasure and the debate.

1 Games people play

Play so you can be serious
ARISTOTLE

There are very few people who eschew all forms of sport and fewer still who claim always to have done so. For the vast majority of us, sport kindles memories of triumphs and tragedies in childhood, adolescence and adulthood; it cloaks a field of dreams. Be it competitive or social, organised or impromptu, a team game or a solo pursuit; whether we dedicate our lives to it or from time to time dip our toes in it, sport touches us all.

But what is 'sport'? George Orwell called it 'war minus the shooting'. And the two have always gone arm in arm. Down the years of history, the words of war have infused the languages of the world. So too have the words and phrases of sport, especially through the media coverage of the last 40 years. We speak of 'goals', 'targets', 'climbing mountains' and 'keeping up to the mark'. Many old and new expressions from sport have to do with violence, aggression and fair play. Perhaps it is because these are as relevant to sport as to war, that they have the same striking impact reflecting dramatic incidents so beloved of the media. From Australian cricket, for example, has come the word 'sledging' – the art of verbal abuse of an opponent. From British rugby came the phrase 'get your retaliation in first' – from the great Welsh coach, Carwyn James, predicting and preparing for aggression from

War minus the shooting?

the All Blacks in 1971. Rugby also gives us 'on the blindside of the referee'. From boxing we get 'hitting after the bell' or 'below the belt'. And from what Peter Tinniswood likes to call the 'summer game' there is perhaps the ultimate description of something unfair or something not quite right – 'it isn't cricket'.

Of course aggression and physical contact are part and parcel of many sports, and players are proud of it. American footballers wear their machismo like a badge. Soccer players talk of 'hard men'. In dressing rooms around the world, at all levels of sport, men and women vow to 'take no prisoners' as they prepare for battle. 'We fought all the way' is the proud boast of the victor or vanquished. And to paraphrase the great French military strategist, Clausewitz, sport surely is meant to be 'the continuation of war by other means'. Sometimes it is meant to hurt and even to draw blood; but always in competition, rather than conflict.

It was the violence in sport that originally led to the formation of rules and to the concept of fair play. These are not modern concerns. In the nineteenth century, public school headmasters in England tried to ban some sports because of their roughness and violence and the too frequent injuries to players. By 1905 the huge toll of death and injury in US college football led President Theodore Roosevelt to intervene, calling college representatives to the White House; Walter Camp was then appointed to advise, and the game was reorganised into the shape and rules we now know.

Today, sport exhibits forms of violence which threaten its future and its past heritage. Sport at the top is serious and increasingly 'professional'. That creed encompasses soccer's 'professional foul' – a sporting euphemism for deliberate and often violent play to halt an opponent and deny him advantage. Harry Catterick, when he was Everton FC's manager in 1971, said, 'Every team has a clogger whose job it is to put a clever opponent out of the match.' Baseball usurped America's early interest in cricket because, as Albert Spalding – one of baseball's earliest advocates – put it, 'cricket is a gentle pastime. Baseball is war!' Tell that to batsmen facing up today to the hostile intimidation of West Indian fast bowling, or to 'sledging' from the Australians. Test cricket now is neither gentle nor a pastime. Jeff Thomson the famous Australian fast bowler said of an opponent 'Let's see how stiff that upper lip is when it's split.' Batsmen used to 'pad up'; now, like American footballers, they don protective clothing from head to toe ready to take the violent blow. Time was when cricketers 'walked' when they knew they were out; they did not wait for the umpire to lift his finger. Such gentle days of sport appear to have gone. Rugby players, like American footballers, train to flatten opponents. In the scrum nasty things happen, although thanks to the special, masonic tradition of these hard men much is often concealed (and resolved without the aid of the referee). In the era of the rugby World Cup, teams have toughened up. Of the England team, for example, an ex-Welsh captain Eddie Butler wrote in June 1991: 'England have swapped "fair play" and "it's only a game" for the cold hearted ruthlessness which is a far better reflection of the Anglo-Saxon soul than the twee virtues shaped by the Victorian forebears of rugby union.'

Some sports, however, consistently set the right example. Golf, snooker, swimming, judo and other martial arts, ice dancing, sumo wrestling, the equestrian sports, fencing and many others maintain standards in competition that enhance rather than reflect those in society. And it is through these sports that we are most easily reminded of sport's original meaning and traditions.

What does sport mean? Generally, it gives us visual rather than word images, and provides us with some of the most powerful pictures of twentieth century society. Sport is theatre, cinema, television and photography, and through these media we can see sport as the human condition cut to the bone. Sport has pace and stillness, drama, comedy and tragedy. It conveys more vividly than any other branch of human activity the elation and despair in everyone's emotional range.

9

Our first and most powerful images are perhaps of sport as 'competition', but only because life, however some may rail against it, is competitive too. For most of us sport is vicarious living. The major sports stage world contests, for which television pays huge sums to bring the drama and entertainment into millions of homes, as well as bars and restaurants and other gathering places, across the earth. This sporting product is immediate, tense, glamorous, and perhaps most importantly, influential in style and manners. It sits atop the strong shoulders of our heroes and heroines and creates history. Jesse Owens *is* the 1936 Olympics and even if few are alive who actually saw a black man thumb his nose at Hitler's Aryan Games, we all know it happened. In a different age, Olga Korbut remains synonymous with gymnastics, years after her mesmerising performance at the 1972 Olympics in Munich has been replaced by later comers.

Even losers can find temporary fame and sometimes even fortune through the universal appeal of sport, as one Olympian, the unsuccessful British ski jumper Eddie Edwards has shown in recent years.

Jesse Owens, the God of the 1936 Olympic Games, an icon of the twentieth century

10

Russia's Olga Korbut, catching the eye of millions at the Munich Olympic Games

Sport is popular with TV and film makers, partly because they know that nothing stops the world in its tracks more effectively. Sport is also cheap compared with many other forms of entertainment. But most of all it attracts massive audiences. Over two hundred million are said to tune in around the world to watch Formula One motor racing on television. A staggering 26.7 billion people overall tuned in to watch the last World Cup in Italy – an average of 513.3 million per game! In the UK alone over 25 million (nearly half the population) watched the semi-final between England and West Germany (95 per cent of the population are said to have seen some of the game!). The bustling city of Buenos Aires was a ghost town when Argentina were playing. Those who could went to home or office or café to watch the games. Those who couldn't huddled in shop doorways within sight of a television set. Scarcely a car moved on the streets. And football is not unique: to a greater or lesser extent baseball, boxing, American football, motor racing, snooker, track and field, *et al*, attract a huge, passionate and dedicated audience.

Television is not yet everything; millions still prefer to 'be there', to be part of, and be close to, the action. From its earliest days, sport was a spectator attraction. Stadium design has changed little since the great Roman architects laid out their temples for entertainment. At their best, grounds and contests have 'atmosphere', the terraces are centres of fun and wit and a collective home for the fans. At their worst, these same grounds and crowds give out the toxic smell of hatred and violence. In soccer, particularly, the last two decades have witnessed outbreaks of 'hooliganism' requiring governmental action and legislation and prompted widespread concern about the proper place of sport in society. 'Hooligans' came into the language in the nineteenth century, but they have been on the terraces for two thousand years.

In almost all sports there is an element of risk; the danger is part of the attraction and the thrill. Some sports and games involve the elements, the great outdoors. People climb mountains and ski down them. There are contests on land, water and snow which test endurance and stamina as well as skill. There are contests of varying kinds with machines where the 'team' includes the designers, builders and mechanics whose 'edge' may swing the contest in a rider's or driver's favour. But it is the player/athlete who takes the risks, and these can be substantial. Danger is part and parcel of many sports; death, tragically, of some. The dangers are very much part of the appeal for competitors and spectators alike.

Other sporting 'teams' involve animals. Horses were in the sporting arena long before the lions. Almost as long as mankind has hunted he has wanted to race. The continued importance of racing today owes much to the gambling industry, but many see beauty as well as excitement in the beast at pace.

Sport is rarely a bland or neutral exercise. It has started at least one war – between Honduras and El Salvador – over a soccer match, but it may also have prevented some. As a release for aggression, it can be cathartic.

Has sport become too big for its boots? Money in those boots has developed international cartels which have secured huge power and influence in certain sports but made no headway at all in others. Sport's gift of fame begets money and prestige and has become indivisible from politics. Governments have taken an interest, sometimes a malign one. Other groups have taken an interest too as we saw to our cost in the terrorist attack at the 1972 Munich Olympic Games.

Some play because they have been inspired by their sporting heroes or heroines, some because it is good for their own health and fitness. Some play for the sense of achievement and some to relieve aggression. All describe it as 'fun' – although it can sometimes look more like pain.

Fundamentally sport is, for all ages and for all reasons, the 'Games people play'. It is 'recreation', or home entertainment, spontaneous or organised, in the club or the company, or between them. Every week and every day millions play in the Global Village – on the street (but rather less than they used to, with modern traffic levels), in the garden, on the sports

field, in the water, in the woods and fields. We play in ones, twos, fours and teams. We play for fun, for passion, for health, for companionship; for ourselves, for the team and forever.

Some of the very top players and athletes can keep it all in perspective. When *wunderkind* Boris Becker, having won the Wimbledon singles for the previous two years, lost in the second round in 1987, he was able to say: 'I haven't lost a war. No one got killed. I just lost a tennis match.'

The Dutch historian, Johan Huizinga, argued that sport's competitive and sometimes aggressive components illustrated our ability to co-operate and to live together harmoniously. Indeed he suggested that playfulness was our most significant characteristic and dubbed us not *Homo sapiens* – wise man, but *Homo ludens* – playful man. The games of sport are an early teaching tool in the home and at school. They help children develop personal qualities of discipline, leadership, teamwork, fair play, responsibility and strategy. They can also help children practise and develop their imagination, individualism and ability under the stress of competition. In most countries, physical education remains a feature of the

No matter how poor the pitch, Cameroons' youngsters have World Cup success to inspire them

14

educational system and provides a seed bed, not just for sport but for the inculcation of personal and cultural values.

The brilliant mathematicians John Von Neumann and Oskar Morgenstern developed a theory about the strategic element of games. 'Game Theory' explores the best move one player can make given the options of his or her opponent. It is more akin to chess than to some sports but the element of strategy is crucial in sport as in life. The 'Game Theory' is fast becoming an essential part of disciplines as diverse as economics, moral philosophy and evolutionary biology.

In this book we examine the different facets of the sporting diamond – a voyage of discovery and development from uncut child to finished, polished, glittering jewel. Sport, we will argue, is a universal language – an Esperanto that unites peoples of every creed, kind and colour. It is very much more than a game.

2 Brown envelopes

Give the Labourer his wage before his perspiration be dry
MUHAMMAD (*c.* 570–632)

When the great statesman, Lord Rosebery, suggested at the turn of this century that the British were becoming 'a nation of amateurs' he was not being complimentary. As a derogatory epithet, 'amateur' sums up all that is feeble minded and inefficient in society. But it also sums up all that is noble, about doing something for the love of it rather than for reward. This contradiction reveals a rift in sport today between the amateur and the professional. The rift is deep.

Life on Earth is based, albeit sometimes loosely, on a system of work for reward. The reward can be spiritual, artistic, physical or material. Money is, increasingly, the normal recompense, and despite their vocational calling, priests, poets, artists and sculptors are little different to solicitors, bankers, engineers, builders and company executives – they all get paid!

There is, however, a view that sport is special and different; that its physical, mental and perhaps even spiritual rewards are all important; and that any financial returns for participants would taint and undermine sport's intrinsic goodness and values. This all-encompassing view is referred to as the 'amateur ethic'. Some sports in particular have defended it vigorously against what they see as a tidal wave of

Gentleman and Players; the bearded W. G. Grace, 'the best paid amateur of all time', with the 1880s England Test team

commercialism and professionalism. But why should sport be different? If talent can usually demand a fee, why is the sportsman or woman treated any different? And why only some of them, when others have fought, and played and performed for money since the earliest days of competition?

In the amateur/professional discussion lie some of the bitterest arguments in sport. Principle is affirmed on both sides. Nowhere is the issue larger than life than in Britain, where much of modern sport began.

The playing of games has always been an important aspect of British society. For centuries before the Industrial Revolution, the mainly rural communities had taken part in a wide range of games with special town or village rules. Market days and agricultural or religious festivals all gave opportunities for contests, usually for enjoyment, although there could be prizes. Community pride was often at stake.

In all this Britain was like countries all round the globe. But with the Victorian age there came a broad spreading of education. Boys mostly, but later girls too, went away and boarded at a range of private establishments which became known as public schools. They commanded high fees and offered severe standards of discipline. Increasing industrialisation drew more and more people into the new urban areas; the cities growing fast with the manufacturing industries. Wealth came to a new group of people later to be called the middle classes, who began to patronise the public schools as part of their upward drift in society.

These public schools had a crucial effect on the development of sport, but it did not happen all at once. The Headmasters of Eton and Winchester tried to ban the early versions of football in the late eighteenth and early nineteenth centuries. Their counterpart at Shrewsbury objected to rowing! Sport was deemed unfit for young gentlemen; it was a rough assembly more suited to the lower classes. But in the 1830s, Dr Thomas Arnold, Headmaster of Rugby school, saw a different side of sport. He recognised and developed its

Football at Rugby school,
England, January 1870

potential for helping young people learn about discipline, pressure, team spirit and playing to rules. (The Rugby School style of football – soon to be called rugby – spread to other schools and influenced the first set of national rules drawn up for the game in 1848.) Arnold's vision was amplified by others. The author and social scientist Charles Kingsley wrote that: 'through sport boys acquire virtues that no books can give them.'

Women were not part of the thinking, even for a social reformer like Kingsley, although women also played and liked sport. Mary Queen of Scots played a form of golf and billiards as early as the sixteenth century; women were seen regularly on the Cresta Run in Saint Moritz in the late 1800s; and in China women played a form of polo during the Tang dynasty (618–907 AD). But women were not yet considered to be serious players and were allowed no place in the control or development of sport.

As the notion of organised sport spread through public schools, it took on a culture and purpose of its own and became part of the curriculum. By the middle of the nineteenth century sporting prowess was a vital asset in the increasingly

Taking sport seriously;
America's Beth Daniel, the
1990 Ladies Professional Golf
Association Player of the Year

19

fierce competition between these schools for new and able pupils. Contrarily, as education spread to the working classes, their schools were usually in urban areas too crowded to allow for playing fields. No playing fields inevitably meant sport assumed lesser importance in the education of the poor. Only gymnastic drill was regularly on offer, and often not as part of the school day; but the tradition of 'community' games continued and football particularly grew apace.

The public schools and the universities provided the originators and custodians of the 'rules' and the key promoters and leaders in many organised games. By and large these were rich young men who didn't need to work, and they founded traditions based more on recreation than reward. The importance of sport in the upbringing of young gentlemen was also enhanced by other cultural, social and scientific developments in the Victorian era. The rural, outdoor life had been left behind, and some of its benefits were missed. In the increasingly crowded cities there were growing concerns about public health; the medical profession was developing rapidly in size and influence; and debate raged about Darwin's theories on the 'survival of the fittest'. Sport and recreation came to be perceived as developing healthy minds and bodies.

The male products of the Victorian public schools and universities spread the word of sport through what was then the huge British Empire, as they travelled across the globe for the army, on business, or as civil servants. The message they carried encompassed the sports themselves and the rules, the codes of conduct and of fair play – everything that was to become enshrined as the 'amateur ethic'. The Victorians believed that gentlemen always behaved well, according to rules of courtesy and self discipline. They knew how to lose, without complaint or protest; how to win with modesty and restraint.

One illustration of the strict notion of fair play comes from the famous amateur soccer club, the Corinthians. Founded in 1882 by N. Lane 'Pa' Jackson, the honorary secretary to the Football Association, to redress Scottish football's supremacy over English, Corinthians drew their numbers from the top public schools and universities. The Corinthians would always withdraw their goalkeeper if they had a penalty awarded against them on the grounds that they should accept the full consequences of their foul play.

There was usually little financial reward for Queen Victoria's successful sportsmen, although schools were not slow to see the added value which sport gave their establishments. But it would be false to imply that sport in those days was completely divorced from money; of course, it was not. Indeed the tradition of prize money and even payment for taking part predates the Victorian public schools.

The Olympic Games, first established in Greece in 776 BC, originally offered only simple garlands of olive leaves to the winners. But even those winners could expect some financial reward back in their home communities and were often paid to appear at local events. Soon, the Games spawned other sporting contests where prizes were given. Such rewards and the prestige brought greater dedication and training, and the first coaches were employed. Some complained of these developments and criticised the system. Galen, a second century AD doctor, spoke of the 'malpractice' of trainers whose 'fraudulent art' produced 'mindless, ugly, distorted men'.

As with the ancient Greeks, so too in Victorian and Edwardian Britain there was a conflict between just taking part, and trying harder and doing better and perhaps being paid for it. In Britain, it was in part a class difference. A distinction became established between 'Gentlemen' (people from the upper or middle class who did not need to work for a living) and 'Players' (from the working class, who certainly did). It was generally acceptable for the latter to receive money for their sporting endeavour – and money was available for football, cricket, horse racing and boxing, in particular. It was less acceptable for the upper and middle classes to be so rewarded. Apart from participating without pay, their role was one of patronage (of working-class sportsmen) and organisation. The upper classes were, however, not averse to betting on anything and everything, from racehorses to prize fighters.

Jack Broughton was an eighteenth-century boxer who made a good living and died a wealthy man. The death of one of his opponents led to boxing's first set of formal rules. His patron was the Duke of Cumberland who once (in 1750) backed Broughton for £10 000 ($20 000). Wagers of £40 000 were known to be placed on fights and crowds of 10 000 attended some contests.

The jockey Tom Cannon was paid a retainer of £15 000 ($72 000) in the 1880s, when the best riders could have earned up to £75 000 in their careers. A Scot named J.J. Lang claimed to be the first ever professional footballer when Sheffield Wednesday apparently paid him to move there from Glasgow, in 1876. In 1900 the governing body, the Football Association, introduced a maximum wage of £4 ($19.50) per week to stop players being lured from one team to another for different sums of money. (The maximum wage rule for footballers in Britain was not abolished until the early 1960s.)

Perhaps in the very English and Empire game of cricket lay the sharpest class distinctions; and here they may have remained the longest. For 150 years this game officially recognised

The great Stanley Matthews, who laboured under British soccer's maximum wage restriction, making magic for Blackpool FC against Chelsea in 1951

'Gentlemen' and 'Players', in gates and entrances, dressing rooms, refreshment areas, and of course money! Naturally, the captain had to be a 'Gentleman'! The first professional, or 'non-Gentleman', to captain England was Len (later Sir Len) Hutton in 1952. But he was never a regular captain of his county, Yorkshire, whose President, Lord Hawke, appealed: 'Pray God that no professional will ever captain Yorkshire.' It was not until 1963 that the English governing body officially abandoned the Gentlemen/Player terms and distinctions.

Arguably the greatest of Britain's sporting heroes was W.G. Grace – a 'Gentleman', in all perhaps but manners and money! Grace dominated English cricket for over 40 years from the 1860s, breaking all records as a batsman and all rounder. He played for England for 19 years (1880–99) and was captain in 13 of his 22 Test matches. He scored nearly 55 000 runs and took nearly 3000 wickets in first class cricket. He also scored well at the bank. At one time, he demanded £20 ($96.50) per match from his team, Gloucester, and he earned the huge sum then of £9000 ($43 400) for his second testimonial. (In 1896 'Players' actually went on strike in pursuit of their demand for £20 per international game or test match.) 'W.G.' was known as 'the best paid amateur of all time'. Although he was the son of a doctor and a doctor himself, Grace was not a product of the public school sporting system. Richard Holt reports in *Sport and the British* that 'the Grace family appear to have done little but play cricket.' The MCC (Marylebone Cricket Club – then the governing body of cricket) could never quite bring themselves to accept him as a 'Gentleman'. In part perhaps it was because of the new work ethic he applied to sport – toiling for long hours practising his skills and techniques – and in part also the equal effort he put in to making sure he was financially rewarded for it. Unlike some gentlemen sportsmen, then as later, and despite a press campaign led by *Punch* magazine, he was never honoured by Queen and country with a knighthood.

Money and fame in sport moved rather faster in the United States. By 1890 college football had become popular,

nationally, developing out of soccer and rugby. Athletics clubs had also emerged; the first, the New York Athletics Club, was formed in 1868. Sporting success enabled young people to enhance their social status. Again, winning became important and the clubs started to pay players to play for them, or to move from one club to another. At first, such payments were secret. The first 'official' and direct payment to an American sportsman – a footballer – was $500 (£103) paid to William Heffelfinger to play for the local Allegheny club in a grudge match against Pennsylvania Athletic Association in 1892. There was outrage when news of the payment surfaced, but such deals continued to be made. In 1883 the first formal professional contract was signed (ironically, by a Pennsylvania player) for $50 (£10) a game. But teams could still be subject to expulsion for being declared wholly 'professional'; and it was not until the 1920s that an official pro-football league came into being.

The change from amateur to professional has dramatically altered the way in to some sports. No one today could wake up in the morning and suddenly decide to enter the Monte Carlo Rally. Thirty years ago anyone could, and did, provided they had the car!

Back in 1947 Paul Zetter was a young Englishman who liked cars and who had just left the war behind him. He had started to work in his father's pools business (the method of gambling on weekly soccer results that has long had a mass following in the UK). Perhaps because his work was in the gambling industry, or maybe because 'Civvy Street' was quiet after the war, Zetter was soon bored. He rather fancied his chances in the Monte Carlo Rally, so he entered. All he needed was a suitable car, and he soon had that – an Allard sports coupé, with a Ford V8 engine which developed 90 bhp. With two friends as co-drivers, his was one of four hundred entries in the first 'Monte' after the war – 1952. Each car had to complete 3500 kilometres in 72 hours, from seven different starting venues throughout Europe. The British start was Glasgow. 'We drove up to Glasgow on the Saturday before

A black and brown study; William Heffelfinger, the first professional footballer in the USA

24

Paul Zetter's Allard arriving in Monaco. No one today could wake up in the morning and enter the Monte Carlo Rally

the Sunday start,' Zetter remembers, 'proudly sporting our two red Monte Carlo Rally plaques with the number 67.' Despite the bitterly cold weather, and no in-car heating of course, they drove with the hood down 'attracting more than our fair share of support'. Zetter's diary records: 'Liège at 1.15am lacks charm' and 'Brussels welcomes us with cheering midday crowds reminiscent of the Liberation.' In France they careered into a lorry near Digne and 'my sadly re-shaped Allard limped ingloriously into Monte Carlo out of luck and out of time'. But out of the four hundred starters, only five had finished within the time, so Zetter and his co-drivers were in good company.

Zetter, who in the late 1970s was to become Chairman of the Sports Aid Foundation in the UK (which raises money to help sports performers develop), competed in four more 'Montes'. But he gave up when the car manufacturers started to employ drivers, and support them with mobile workshops. 'The days of the amateur were over, and I had to put it all behind me.'

Nowadays motor racing is a strictly professional business, though amateurs still cling to the fringes with old banger stock cars, with special formula races and with go-karts. The real thing is strictly for professionals, and not just because of the costs involved. At top speeds of over 200mph, today's grand prix circuits are not for weekend drivers!

In some ways, sport is a victim of its own success. It has become not just big business, but one of the biggest in the world. Increased competition and greater rewards bring their own pressures, and raise new arguments. Competitors devoting all their time to sport must be able to earn a living from it, directly or indirectly.

Top performers know that the crowds pay to see them. They recognise that it is their skills and the drama of their matches which the TV companies pay to screen; it is their exploits and opinions that sell newspapers and magazines. Performers are aware, too, that the sporting life is short. Unlike lawyers, plumbers or TV commentators for that matter, they cannot expect to work until the age of 60 or 65 and then take a comfortable pension. Sportsmen and women have to make the most of a short, explosive career cycle, with its attendant hazards of injury and luck.

Few could fault the rationale of Jean-Claude Killy, the champion French skier, saying (in 1972) that there were no amateurs any more. 'To be good', he argued, 'a skier must

Jean-Claude Killy; have skis, will travel, need money

26

literally devote four to six years of his life to the sport. You don't have time for a school or a job and you must travel the world. That's hard to do without compensation.'

Over the last 40 years the administrators of several sports have fought to keep to the amateur ethic and to retain the traditional approach, values and procedures. But, in most, they have not managed to stem the tide of the pro taking over at the top of the game. In tennis, for example, there was a long delay in the 1950s and 60s in the introduction of Open tennis. The All England Club at Wimbledon at last opened its manicured grass courts to professionals in 1968, forced eventually by falling standards of play. The best players, like Laver, Hood and Rosewall, had turned professional; without them and the other professionals the Wimbledon tournament, which is so much a part of the British sporting and social season, had become second rate. Now, market forces operate in tennis. The few who are good enough can enter tournaments and justify being paid to entertain the rest of us, while the vast majority of tennis players in the world remain amateur, and happily so.

Another sport beset with conflicts over money for top performers was athletics. Track and field has been the major Olympic sport throughout the modern era and has consistently attracted great public interest. World record holders are fêted in most countries, and television made an early beeline for athletics contests. But as the money grew, the athletes themselves received little. Not all of them cared. Perhaps the greatest track star of the 1950s, Emil Zatopek of Czechoslovakia, argued that 'an athlete cannot run with money in his pockets. He must run with hope in his heart and dreams in his head.' In the 1960s and 70s most world class athletes began to expect the money in their pockets and largely to preserve the amateur status of the sport, it came in cash in 'brown envelopes' rather than by cheque or bank draft.

Seb Coe remembers the last days of this particular Raj. When first an international athlete he would only receive a second class rail ticket and a meal voucher. His career in athletics straddled a period of rapid change for both the sport and its funds. Athletes received 'expenses' worked out more on how good they were rather than how far they had travelled. Although 'expenses' were to grow handsomely for the top achievers, the principles of amateurism were stoutly maintained by the sport's leaders. Their language would not have been out of place in the last century. It was vital, they argued, that sport was pursued for its own sake, and for its intrinsic benefits to the individual and the community.

Seb Coe's first 'expenses' came in Brussels in 1976, when they weren't over-generous: 'I remember running 1.46 in the 800 metres and then arguing over the exchange rate because it made the difference between £98 and £104!'

Seb Coe, flying the flag, Los Angeles, 1984

In the next few years payments like these were made in cash in hotel rooms, at a trestle table outside the canteen or even in the car park. 'It wasn't a system that most of us were happy with. It forced honest people to act dishonestly – according to the strict rules then of the sport.' But money had become essential to the development of the sport, especially in quality of performance. Coe's rationale is no different from Killy's: 'There is and was no greater thrill than pulling on my country's vest, whether for England or Great Britain. That thrill has not diminished. But to get to that top level, and to stay there for 14 years, I had to commit myself to the sport. That was not compatible with advancing a normal career.'

Increasingly, top class sportsmen and women agree. Ed Moses, the American 400 metres hurdler, says of the amateur system: 'It is an insult to my ego and intelligence. It's insulting to me to have to exist like this. People in sport feel like they're doing something illegal just trying to survive.' Another black American athelete, the sprinter Carl Lewis, puts it more forcefully: 'We have to cut out all this amateur crap; it's phony! We have to be openly professional, money on the table where everybody can see it.'

In 1981 a classic compromise was reached which allowed athletes to receive money openly without upsetting the amateur status of their sport. The money could be paid to a trust fund from which the athlete could take out 'living expenses'. These would cover the expectations of most working people in providing mortgages, motor cars, holidays, even private schooling, a dishwasher or a chauffeur; in other words all the other things on which the rest of us might choose to spend our salaries, if large enough!

A major dam, however, remains in the sport of rugby union, in Great Britain at least. Administrators in that sport contend that the majority of rugby players wish to keep it amateur. Again, the old arguments surface, about traditions and principles, about sport for its own sake. And again the players grow frustrated watching money piles grow through their efforts and remain firmly out of their reach.

Dudley Wood, Secretary of the (English) RFU (Rugby Football Union) has frequently claimed that he gets most applause at any rugby gathering for any statement reaffirming the policy of 'keeping the game amateur'. Those who applaud in clubhouses around the country are perhaps not the ones having to train, practise and play virtually full time; and they are not the élite few whose exploits fill the game's shop window. In any event, there appears to be no consistency. Back in 1974 the great New Zealand scrum half and captain, Chris Laidlaw was already saying 'any rugby player worth his salt in France who does not accept payment is considered a fool and a rare one at that.' In New Zealand and Australia now, a number of players are being paid handsomely – professionals in all but name. Wayne Shelford, the New Zealand captain, is a case in point. His major source of income derives from speaking engagements, TV commentaries, promotions and so on; all the contracts arise from his achievements on the field of play and his status as a hugely successful international player. Both the International Rugby Union Board and the New Zealand Rugby Union have not prevented Shelford's activities, and he is of course not unique.

Resistance, though, has continued, even from the players themselves. The amateur camp argues that any form of professional status leads to a 'win at all costs' attitude, and thus to rough or violent play, to gamesmanship, and so on. Bill Beaumont, the prop forward who led England to their Grand Slam victory (against Scotland, Wales, Ireland and France) in 1980, says 'money would probably have made me a dirtier player.' In his autobiography *Thanks to Rugby* Beaumont says 'I have always believed that no one should ever receive money for actually playing rugby ... it would ruin the game itself and the whole structure of rugby in Britain.' What saddened Beaumont though was the inflexibility of the rules applying after a player had retired. Earning his living writing and commentating on the game has changed his status within rugby, and he said: 'I find it sad that I am now branded a professional for life and forbidden ever to coach or help in the administration of a club or county side – in short to put anything back into the game that has given me so much.' In 1990 the RFU changed its mind, and Beaumont can now coach amateur players. That battle over, the war continues (at the time of writing) although it may be resolved at the second rugby union World Cup (to be staged in Britain and France in Autumn 1991). British players have united in a proposal for a campaign called 'Play The Ball', designed to publicise and develop the game and to make some legitimate money for the players.

The great Australian fly half, Michael Lynagh, has resisted big offers to turn professional with rugby league. He said in May 1991: 'sometime we will be paid for playing, but it can only be at international level. There's just not the money lower down.' A good club match only attracts small crowds of 1500 or so. But already he gets paid for a newspaper column on rugby, a privilege denied to British players. It remains to be seen whether a workable compromise can be reached. Most rugby players are adamant they want to remain 'amateurs', not in the strict Victorian sense but in performing for free and for fun. They do, however, want to be able to earn outside the game, through the endorsements and sponsorship arrangements commonplace in other sports.

Jonathan Davies was captain of Wales and the latest in their tradition of great outside halves, but he turned professional to play rugby league in England in 1988. He told us that some compromise to allow earnings outside the rugby union game would have kept him in the amateur camp. He turned down offers with various kinds of 'incentive' from rugby union clubs in England, France and Italy. Davies says: 'I've never advocated being paid for playing and even now, as a professional, it's pride in performance and not money that motivates me on the field. There is far more money in rugby union than league, but only in the league does any of it go to the players. But top union players have to commit themselves – at the top it's 90 per cent preparation and only 10 per cent participation. And we all have families to support and futures to think about.' Davies is convinced too at the clear evidence of different attitudes to the international rugby rules: 'You could drive a bus through the regulations in some countries.'

The Welsh valleys, and the national team, have still not recovered from his loss! And few would argue with another legendary Welsh player, Vivian Jenkins, later to become an eminent sportswriter, who said: 'The only real amateur is one who pays his own expenses.'

Today, the test for most sports and for events like the Olympic Games is 'eligibility'; this is defined by specific rules. So, except in cases like rugby union the word 'amateur' has passed from common parlance.

Not everyone is satisfied with the way things have turned out in sport. Philippe Chatrier presided for 14 years over international tennis, a period when its management became as professional as the game. Now he believes there is too much money around and this is seriously affecting young players. 'Every morning when I get up,' he told us, 'I see something I don't like in the game.'

No less an authority than Prince Philip, President of the Central Council of Physical Recreation in Britain and a former President of the International Equestrian Federation, said in 1986 he thought money the most 'corroding influence' in sport. 'Money changes the whole perspective and brings in a completely new range of motives and considerations.'

It is certainly true that standards of behaviour cause proper anxiety in many sports – to players, administrators and sponsors. But the relationship to money and prizes is more complicated. Tennis, athletics and rugby union each have plenty of evidence of 'unsportsmanlike' behaviour in genuinely amateur competition. The McEnroe brat image is now a familiar one in tennis clubs; sharp elbows appear on the school running track with depressing regularity; the Sunday morning soccer pitch is rife with bad language and bad play. But at the same time, golf, one of the first games to embrace professionals (and produce some of the top sports earners) maintains exemplary behaviour on and off the greens.

It is reasonable to ask whether effective coaching and management of young sportsmen and women, allied to decisive leadership, would have a greater impact upon discipline and fair play than restrictions on financial rewards. In so far as many sports today attract huge audiences, sponsorships and media attention, it is clear they must be managed in a businesslike fashion. Preventing top performers earning a reasonable share of the wealth they help to create is unreasonable, and the history of the last 20 years shows that such barriers to trade cannot be maintained indefinitely. Sport needs a businesslike approach, but it is not just another business in the marketplace. It will never be that; it has an appeal beyond monetary reward, and offers honours and prizes that cannot be valued in marketplace terms. Administrators have a duty to encourage and spread the practise of sport for all those old values and benefits advertised by the public schools in the last century. The amateur ethic is still alive and well; and it applies happily to the great majority of those millions enjoying sport around the world today.

The writers of this book all believe that sport is special; and

Leader of the Brat Pack;
McEnroe v umpire

so it has special needs and responsibilities. Sport has to practise a mixed economy, with an honest balance of professionals and amateurs reflecting the different levels and appeals of different sports. As we have already seen the balance is not easy to strike.

3 The search for a champion

He just had a God gifted ability that we have never seen in America in one individual

ART STEWART, KANSAS CITY ROYALS SCOUT,

TALKING ABOUT BO JACKSON

No word which has passed from sporting into everyday parlance has more powerful connotations than the word 'champion'. The *Oxford Dictionary* defines it as 'a fighting man; a stout fighter' and 'one who has defeated all opponents in any trial of strength or skill ...'

Each generation recalls its own heroes etched indelibly in the mind – aided once by ballad or painting and now by photograph and videotape – Pele and Stanley Matthews in soccer; Don Bradman in cricket; Olga Korbut, a gymnast supreme; Babe Ruth in baseball; Joe Namath in American football and Bo Jackson in both baseball and football. No list will be identical, but some names will appear on almost everyone's: Daley Thompson, Emil Zatopek, Carl Lewis in athletics; Muhammad Ali for boxing; Fred Perry, Chris Evert or Bjorn Borg in tennis; Barry John, Eddie Merkx, Lester Piggott, Juan Fangio, Jean-Claude Killy and many, many more. They are the champions and champions are the stuff of dreams.

The champion is the best, and even at local level they are not discovered by chance. In modern times at least, but

The 'Time Lord' of champions: Daley Thompson with the field at his feet; European Championships, 1982

35

probably always, champions are made not born. To be a sporting champion at any significant level requires a long apprenticeship plus skill, effort, commitment and help. It also requires time, for the expertise to develop and for the opportunities to arise. Seb Coe is not being modest when he underlines how important a factor is opportunity; many great sporting performers have failed to be champions because they missed the right slot in the sporting schedule.

The search for a champion is a three phase odyssey; finding them, training them, and finally allowing them to get it right in the arena. Those who make it are those prepared to make the ultimate personal sacrifices for their sporting goals.

The identikit of a champion has one essential component – the ability to win. It is the most precious commodity in competitive sport; the knack, the character, the innate sense, the ability to concentrate skills and effort at the right time and place set for a particular championship and thus to emerge the victor.

Most of us can recognise a champion when we see one. Usually, it is obvious; a winner is declared, an opponent is knocked out, a team collects most points. But it is a rare talent to recognise a champion early, before prime is reached, and especially before the champions themselves know it. That is the forte of the coach, manager or selector – a mixture of art and science, foresight, experience and not a little luck.

Everywhere the search for a champion starts with children. With certain notable exceptions like shooting and yachting, sport is a young persons' pursuit; gymnastics and swimming are for very young people indeed. At eight years of age, for example, the would-be world class gymnast has to be close to the finished product. Talent has to be spotted early, although there are famous late-developers. The British 400 metres hurdles 1968 Olympic gold medallist, David Hemery, himself something of a late-developer, argues in his book, *Sporting Excellence*, that children should not specialise too quickly and should take time to develop themselves in the right sport or event. But Hemery is very much in the minority.

The champion, Martina Navratilova. She was found and trained in Czechoslovakia, honed in the USA and world arena

What does a coach look for? Peter Coe, father of (and coach to) Sebastian says the first imperative is 'style'. He defines this as 'all the movements co-ordinated to produce the elegance and efficiency appropriate to the particular discipline'. The basis is the old engineering dictum that 'if it looks right, it probably is right'. The second question is whether the boy or girl can be taught; has he or she the readiness and the aptitude? Third, Peter Coe tries to look into the 'inner self'. How do they perceive themselves? As successful, or not? And finally, has the individual the necessary discipline? Peter Coe looks for 'a bloody-minded determination to succeed'.

All over the United States, young hopefuls sifted from school go to summer baseball camps, to be scrutinised by professional coaches anxious to augment their stables. It's a first step to stardom in America's national game. Tom Burgess, hitting coach for Kansas City Royals, looks for bat speed and balance. 'I don't see the upper part of (his) body. It's from the waist down, his approach into the strike zone, that's the area I focus on in most hitters.'

We watched Tom Burgess with a young batter, Darren Burton, an 18-year-old, from Somerset, Kentucky, a six foot two outfielder with a toothbrace. He is outstandingly quick to first base, and Burgess believes the young Burton is a man to steal bases. He has already been chosen for the local All Star team, and Burgess believes the youngster can make it to the top. So does Joe Jones, the overall coaching co-ordinator, who reckons Burton has skills 'in a lot of different areas. He's a fast runner, he has a good strong arm, he bats from both sides of the plate which is what we call a switch-hitter. He can hit left handed and right handed and he has time on his side because he's just out of high school.' Interestingly, and crucially, Jones told us that the young Burton 'also has a tremendous work ethic! I think you'll see him in the big leagues within four years or so.'

The Royals take their search for baseball talent seriously. The club has about 140 coaches in the minor leagues and around the schools, looking for and coaching the future talent.

The prospect; Darren Burton, at Kansas City Royals baseball camp

Burgess told us: 'There's a tremendous amount of money expended at the minor league level, and I'm talking two, three, four million dollars that is spent (there) alone ... that's big business.' At the camps the prodigies undergo training and selection along military lines. The best mature and go on into well-paid careers, but most will have to find other ways to earn their living. Another Kansas coach said of the 40 hopeful young men in front of him; 'maybe two or three of those guys actually have the makings of a big league pitcher.'

Such decisions are far from straightforward. Coaches, like selectors, must be prepared to be shown up as mugs or fools. So much can go wrong, or right, in a young person's physical and mental development. The pacy 14-year-old can be slow for life four years later, because of the way his or her limbs have grown. The 16-year-old with sublime skills and effortless vision may be fatally distracted within two or three years by the other charms of life.

There are, though, general guidelines which apply everywhere to the selection of talent. The most obvious is geographic; even today, it matters where you are born. Wales has its factory for outside halves, as Kenya has its running school. Australians wouldn't give much for success in sports other than their own rules of football, cricket and rugby. Every country has its own traditions that are hard to break. Although soccer is the fastest growing sport in the USA, and the 1994 World Cup is to be staged there, the usual opportunities are not available yet for young footballers. The competition does not exist; there is no coaching or career structure. For a while yet any talent is likely to wither on the Californian vine. Conversely, of course, it would be very difficult really to excel at baseball in any country other than the USA, with the possible exception of Japan which has become the main centre for baseball outside America. And outside Japan it would be hard indeed to get to the top in Sumo wrestling! Much of it has to do simply with resources – the availability of facilities and equipment varies enormously.

Baseball diamonds are plentiful in the USA, as are cricket squares and nets in England and table tennis tables in China.

Another environmental factor is wealth and its cousin, class. Twenty years ago, what Britain's *Sunday Times* called the 'cathedral calm of the croquet world' was shattered by an argument over who should be encouraged to play. In support of claims that the wrong kind of people might be brought into the game as a result of using public money to promote it, the then chairman of the Croquet Association in England, S.S. Townsend argued that 'a high degree of skill and intelligence are required for croquet, and therefore it is not going to attract the lower income groups.' He was to apologise shortly afterwards, but then, as now, background and what it represents are important indicators in some sports. An Irish American builder called John Kelly was an Olympic champion oarsman from the Antwerp Games in 1920, but he still found himself barred from the prestigious Henley Royal Regatta in England that year, because of his class. (Ironically his daughter, Grace, later became Princess Grace of Monaco.)

Sport has long been a way out of the poverty trap. It has fed 'hungry' fighters and footballers, but perhaps not croquet players or show jumpers. The American baseball legend, Joe Di Maggio, said: 'A ball player's got to be kept hungry … that's why no boy from a nice family ever made the big leagues.' On the other hand, equestrian sports tend only to be open to those who can afford the maintenance of its horses, and it is impossible to break into motor racing without considerable financial support.

The sifting process is more rigorous and efficient in some countries. The East Germans made what some would consider a fetish of it; with a combination of rigidly efficient selection and drug enhanced training, they changed the records books in the 1970s and 80s. The Chinese put all their children through National Standards of Physical Fitness Tests during school time, with a network of special facilities for sports leading to 'Key Sports Schools' for the exceptionally talented. Craig Lord reported in the British newspaper *The Times* in

Practising at the bar; four young Chinese girls selected for training

1991 that Chinese children as young as eight train for up to four hours a day in preparation for Olympic, World and Asian games. 'They are very well looked after. They have a better life than they might at home.' There was a similar system in the USSR, which is creaking under political developments at the moment. In the UK a major study, TOYA (the Training of Young Athletes), funded by the Sports Council is examining the impact of special training for sport on youngsters and attempting to assess the costs and the benefits.

In the late 1970s the Australian government decided that it had a legitimate role in actively assisting the development of sporting talent in Australia. The result was the Institute of Sport in Canberra. In the mid 1980s the senior official in the Australian government responsible for the institute visited his opposite numbers in the UK Minister of Sport's office. But their standard re-active, rather than pro-active role, precluded anything more than the usual 'Good to listen to you; we'll pass your material on to our agency, the Sports Council' response. The Canberra funds have come mainly from the government, with the declared aim of helping the development of sporting champions and thus to enhance the nation's

40

prestige. The French have a similar centre at Vincennes, again aided by public money. Neither of these projects has yet established a tradition of success, but it is clear that they do attract young talent within the countries concerned. In Germany they have changed some traditions. It is no accident that the 1991 Wimbledon Men's Singles Final was played between two Germans, and German ladies won the Women's Singles and Junior titles. The success comes from good facilities and coaching, and an eye for a young player.

There is nothing special in the air around Bruhl in Germany, but the *Verbandtrainer* (regional tennis coach) has a very keen eye for promising young players. Boris Becker and Steffi Graf both came from here, as did Anke Huber, about whom we should hear a lot more in the future. Tennis in Germany is much more systematically organised than in other countries. According to Norbert Rogenkamp, of the *Deutcher TennisBund* (DTB – German Tennis Association), this is possibly because Germany 'discovered tennis relatively recently and had to create from scratch new playing facilities, training patterns and financing'. Ever since Becker made his surprise appearance in the Wimbledon Final in 1985, tennis has been big business in Germany. A game which used not to be played in schools and universities, nor much in parks and private homes, tennis has grown to become second only to football in popularity.

As with politics and education, sport is organised within the federalist framework of *Bundeslander* (autonomous regions). Each *Bundesland* will hold regional tournaments for which local schools and clubs will be on the lookout for potential talent. Names will be forwarded to *Bundestrainers* (national coaches) who spend considerable time travelling around the country checking out those talents. From the age of 16, promising players will be sponsored by the DTB under the tuition of the national coaches. It seems a fair bet that Germany will be a force in world tennis for some time to come. It is also no coincidence that the biggest new tennis tournament, the Grand Slam Cup, now takes place in Munich.

Sport used to be full of shibboleths of an environmental kind. In the 1960s it was said that Australians and Americans must always dominate tennis because they had the climate, courts and traditions. It is many years now since there was an Australian champion and the Americans are far from dominating world tennis; the best players are from Sweden, Czechoslovakia, and as we have indicated, Germany. It was said that the best golfers would always be American. Now, Europeans have regularly won the major titles around the world.

So any country or nationality can produce top sports people, of any discipline. But traditions are important because they usually mean that facilities and equipment, hero and heroine role models, and coaches and coaching systems, are readily available.

The second phase in the odyssey is, if anything, even more crucial than the first. Having identified promising talent there comes the coaching – that period of teaching and learning, of practice and development, of unstinting hard work, which will turn a very few into champions. Surprisingly, the TOYA study suggests that while a child's initial interest in a particular sport depends usually on the parent, it is the youngsters themselves who push towards more intensive training.

In the public mind, this can be a process of painful perseverance and near monastic obsession. These images derive mainly from athletics and may have started with the regimes of the great Arthur Lydiard in the 1950s and 60s. His hard, physical training produced two champions, Peter Snell (800 metres) and Murray Halberg (5000 metres) in the space of an hour at the 1960 Olympic Games in Rome. Snell later did the 800 metres and 1500 metres double at the 1964 Games. Another Lydiard athlete, John Davies, took the 1500 metres bronze at the same Games. Lydiard also influenced coaches and athletes (including John Walker) around the world. Lydiard had Snell running marathons uphill in his late teens. The process undoubtedly produced results. Remarkably,

Lydiard always undertook the same training sessions as his athletes, for example running alongside Snell in those marathons. When Seb talked to him in New Zealand in 1990 he said he still runs twice a day, although he is in his seventies.

Coaching regimes vary by sport and by region, although in these days of mass media and communication there are fewer and fewer secrets. Environmental factors also impinge on coaching. Given what we have said about German tennis, why has no British man made it to the final since the great Fred Perry in the mid 1930s; and no woman since Virginia Wade in 1977? This is despite the annual tournament at Wimbledon, which has such a place in the national psyche, or it is perhaps because of Wimbledon, which is undoubtedly a bear pit of extra pressure for home grown talent. For Ion Tiriac, the famous Romanian coach, the cause is simple. He told us that in Britain 'you don't have coaches technically capable of taking a kid to world rankings'. When Olga Morozova, Wimbledon finalist in 1974 and six times the Soviet Women's Champion, took over coaching British girls in 1990 she said 'the first thing I have to teach them is that they can win.' Of her 13-year-old charges at the Bisham Abbey Centre of Excellence, she says 'We must open their eyes, give belief.' She says the problem is 'to find the ones with the right spirit.' Tiriac believes change in Britain's tennis will not be easy. 'In Germany, I ask a kid like Boris Becker to jump and he asks how high? In Britain they ask why?'

British players have noted the difference in Germany in sport and investment. Andrew Davies, a British Davies Cup player, commented in 1991: 'The reality is you are on your own. The German Federation invested more in Becker than the Lawn Tennis Association spent on the coaching programme for the south east of England.'

In the UK, one of the longest established coaching systems is in the English Football League. For 30 or 40 years league clubs have taken young players on to their staff as 'apprentices' and given them menial jobs, like cleaning boots, or grandstands, while providing coaching and playing opportunities.

43

A lot of the costs are actually now borne by the government, since many of the apprentices come on government training and work experience schemes. Bertie Mee was the manager of London's famous Arsenal Football Club, renowned for developing young talent, and won the elusive 'Double' (Championship and Cup) in 1971. Mee made a careful study of Arsenal's success rate with apprentices from 1960 to 1970; over 100 apprentices passed through his hands. 'About a third of them,' he says, 'made their living in the game at some level; a third dropped out because of lack of ability, medical problems and other miscellaneous reasons; and one third failed because of attitude problems or lack of discipline.' Mee's analysis suggests that of the third staying in the game perhaps 6 or 8 per cent would reach international level. 'Only one in two hundred become real champions, of world class, and they are readily identifiable at the age of 14 or 15.'

Mee also examined the cost of the Arsenal system. In any season in the period studied, the club's scouts would see around 80 000 young players in 4000 games. In any one year only about 40 were invited to Arsenal's famous ground at Highbury, North London, for a detailed appraisal and on average 10 of those then joined as apprentices. Only one every two years, on average, made it as a first division footballer. The cost of developing one first division player was calculated at £60 000 (1968 figures), compared with the average transfer fee at the time of £100 000 ($239 000) or more.

Back at the Kansas City Royals baseball camp, in 1991, the coaches reckoned between 4 and 6 per cent would make it as major league players. Tom Burgess, the hitting coach, told us the coaching team 'will have done a fine job' at that rate. He agreed with Bertie Mee that buying players on the transfer market is more costly than 'finding them yourself'. Moreover, 'youngsters we can train and mould into the ball players we want.'

For many people, including the authors of this book, Daley Thompson is a 'Time Lord' of champions. His record of championship success between 1978 and 1988 may remain

44

unequalled for a very long time. He was first identified at secondary school as a winner of a Five Star Athletic Award, a scheme run by athletics' governing bodies in conjunction with schools as a means of encouraging young athletes. Once identified, much work was done with him in the middle 1970s on the various parts of the decathlon discipline. He was a natural sprinter and jumper, but needed to learn from scratch the discus and pole vault.

Even champions have to learn how to put spin on a ball; it doesn't all come naturally. Which fiend, after all, would imagine that getting a small ball out of a pit of deep sand required any of life's natural skills? A prospective champion needs to broaden and expand what he or she does naturally, and learn a little more besides. With Sebastian Coe, it was his arm action. For Steve Backley, a javelin world record holder, the emphasis was on throwing technique to achieve maximum efficiency. For James Hunt, the 1980 world champion racing driver, the need was to temper his daring with the caution and what is called 'risk percentage assessment' required to last the Grand Prix courses. (In his apprenticeship he was known as 'Hunt the Shunt' for his frequent accidents.) David Hemery was converted by his coach to a completely different event – from the high hurdles sprint to the 400 metres hurdles – and thus found his 'champion' event and a world record at the Mexico Olympic Games in 1968.

Modern coaching practices are not very different from modern management techniques. Developing a sporting champion is fundamentally the same process as producing a top performer in any field, or indeed developing and launching a new product or policy. Some of the mystique around sport is false, or misleading, or even self deceiving.

Like any good business plan, the first step will be to agree general and specific objectives; for example, the Olympic title four or eight years hence, a baseball World Series perhaps three years ahead, and the intermediate aims *en route*. There will also be measurable objectives for specific changes in the player/athlete's skills, technique and performance – expressed

45

perhaps as seconds off a time, inches on a distance or height, or as alterations/improvements in the player's stock of skills like full use of the wrong foot, or a longer pass. Next, a detailed plan must be drawn up to achieve those objectives within a given timescale. Abdi Bile, the Somalian 1988 Olympic gold medallist in the 1500 metres, says 'It doesn't matter how little it is (or) what it is; if you come up with a plan, and you have the training, you just have to believe in what you do.' Any plan must be monitored, to note the progress against the measured targets, and revised as necessary. Finally, the objectives are also reviewed and amended according to progress.

Ron Clarke, the Australian world record distance runner in the 1960s, took the planning process very seriously earlier than most, and gained supreme confidence from his preparation. 'I found I wanted to race because I knew that I'd done more training than anyone else, and better training than anyone else, and I wanted to test that in a race. And I wanted to make them run hard in a race to see just how good they were *vis à vis* the background I'd prepared myself on.'

Part of this management process of development overlaps with the third and final phase in our search – the performance itself. Champions can only be developed through testing themselves against others, at different levels and places. To get to the Superbowl, any great quarterback has thrown his passes at least a thousand times. The top snooker player has tested his talent through hundreds of frames in competition, as well as in practice.

It is in the arena that champions are finally made – as well as crowned. The world is full of near champions, who were unable to perform in the spotlight of the packed stadium. Seb Coe's view, like his father's is that the mental confidence and strength to produce the best when the best is needed is the key attribute of the champion performer. Steve Ovett, Seb's great rival, said of him: 'On the day and time that matters, Coe is the one to watch.' On the day, all the coach can do is watch as well. Peter Coe's view is that 'on the day, I'm a valet.'

When Bill Veeck, the owner of the Cleveland Browns baseball team in the United States, said 'I do not think winning is the most important thing, I think it's the only thing,' he was simply enunciating what sportsmen and women, millions of fans, even nations themselves, believe. The aim of sport is to win.

The overriding will to win generates its own force. Jonah Barrington, who dominated British squash in the 1970s illustrates it better than most. 'At squash,' he says, 'there is a fantastic and savage and unrivalled and unbelievable satisfaction at the moment you know you have beaten your opponent. There is simply no feeling on earth like it – it is a primitive thing, a conquest, an utter victory. You look into his eyes and you see the defeat there, the degradation, the humiliation, the beaten look and there isn't anything in the world like it.'

In some sports, particularly team games, there is a lot the coach can do from the sidelines, and nowhere more so than in American football. Coaches can change the team structure for offence and defence. They have two-way radios to call 'plays' to the quarterback. They call 'time out' when they perceive an advantage in having a break, whether for a rest, for advice, motivation or simply to interrupt the other side's rhythm.

Nowhere is the status of the coach greater than in the closed environs of an American university. We were told that Bobby Knight, basketball coach at Indiana State, 'could run for Governor and win' if the university won the (national) championship this year. Whatever his political ambitions, Knight is regarded as one of the great modern 'motivational' coaches in any sport; he is also one of the loudest and most vociferous. Indiana State, at Bloomington, about an hour's journey from Indianapolis, is the automatic choice for tall basketball-playing middle-class boys from all over the state and beyond. Knight coached the American men's basketball team for the 1984 Olympics, which, as they are fond of saying in Bloomington, 'is the last time they won'! At Indiana State he has

47

worked a similar spell, finding the right players and moulding them into highly motivated squads. He has taken them to three national championships. 'You'll learn as much about life on the basketball court as you will for the rest of your degree,' Knight tells his students.

Watching him at a game is like looking at a pressure cooker boiling; at any moment it might explode. He is alternately blaspheming, coaxing, cajoling, pleading, promising and threatening his charges to perform to his standards. He's been known to throw a chair and a few other things besides, but he does achieve some astonishing results. During the 1991 NCAA (National Collegiate Athletic Association) regional finals at Louisville, Kentucky, the Indiana State 'Hoosiers' looked well and truly beaten at the end of the first half against Florida State. After a talking to by Knight they went back on and started the second half with a 21–2 run. Throughout the half they had no turn-overs (when the ball is accidentally given to the other side) and eventually won 82–60. All the experts watching thought it was as good a demonstration of a coach's ability to lift a team as you could hope to see.

Whatever, and however, the coach performs, he or she is part of a team which depends on confidence and trust. Athletes and players have to believe in themselves, and to do that effectively, they have to believe in their coaches. Franz Stampfl, the Austrian who coached runners like Roger Bannister and Chris Chataway in the 1950s, described his role as '20 per cent technical and 80 per cent inspirational'. There is a bond which Stampfl called 'confidence and comradeship' between player and coach. The good coach can renew that bond, that mutual determination to win, in the heat of the competition whether he or she is there in person on the touchline or not.

Some coaches believe that their role is finished once the contest has begun. In Britain a famous exponent of this view is Brian Clough, manager of Nottingham Forest football club. Clough was much criticised after the 1991 FA Cup Final because he didn't go on to the pitch to counsel his team

48

before extra-time was played. (Nottingham Forest lost 1–2 to Tottenham Hotspur.)

Bertie Mee believes that a´ top international side, one capable of winning FIFA's World Cup, needs five or six world class soccer players in a team of 11 and a squad usually of 22. 'In 1966 the England side had five such players – Banks, Moore, Peters, Charlton and Hurst – and became champions. But in the 1990 World Cup, we had only one or perhaps two. There is a chemistry that binds a great team that is a mixture of great individual players and their collective coaching, and perhaps a dose of luck which finds them together at the right time.'

The Emperor Napoleon used to ask his potential generals whether they were lucky. Sporting champions also need some luck. The weather and the toss of a coin remain influential, affecting surfaces, ends, and directions. The wind is capricious, the sun has no favourites, the rain like the tide waits for no one. The best preparation can't always prevent a torn muscle, still less a car accident.

Champions are found, developed and then enabled and encouraged to perform. All are born with natural ability which is honed and harnessed. The greats are usually those with the most talent who therefore make the least demands on their coaches. Jesse Owens, for example, had the enduring talent to set a world record of 9.4 seconds for the 110 yards at the age of 17 (a record that stood for 21 years) and to run the same distance in 9.8 seconds when 43 years old.

But many have talent, and simply cannot perform. The search for a champion casts a wide net and only a few make the grade; they are like the small specks of true gold left after the prospector's pan has been shaken hard and shaken again, and again. 'There is no one secret,' Joe Jones, senior coach at Kansas City Royals, told us, 'it's a matter of signing the best talent available and working hard with them.'

In Kansas, as all over America, they talk with reverence, even awe, about Bo Jackson, who has reached the very top in not one but two major American sports – baseball and

Dual hitter; Bo Jackson, incomparable at football for LA Raiders or baseball for Kansas City Royals

50

American football. He was a left fielder for the Kansas City Royals and, in football, running back for the Los Angeles Raiders. He is the only player to have been selected for All Star teams in both games; the most celebrated, maybe the greatest figure in American sport. Art Stewart, the Scouting Director for the Kansas City Royals, calls him, without embarrassment, 'probably the most gifted athlete in our century'. Stewart told us 'he did things that we've never seen in baseball. No matter where we went and played, he packed the ball parks because of that charisma, there was a certain presence about him.' Jackson did spectacular things in football too, a superstar just as he was in baseball and one of the fastest runners ever in the game. 'Once he got out (into the open),' Stewart says, 'they couldn't catch him. This past year he broke through for a 98 yard touchdown; in another game 99 yards. Twice in one season, never happened before.'

Good as he was, when Jackson sustained a bad injury playing football for the Los Angeles Raiders earlier in 1991, he was dropped from both the Kansas City Royals and the Los Angeles Raiders, and his contracts were torn up. In sport in particular, memories last a lot longer than careers. Herk Robinson, the General Manager told us 'Our business is a very tough business. It's a very cruel business at times.'

John McEnroe, the tennis player most people love to hate, and sometimes wish they could emulate says, 'The fact is that everyone has their time. Then you don't have it anymore.'

51

4 Body and soul

Athletes live a life quite contrary to the precepts of hygiene and I regard that mode of living as a regime more favourable to illness than to health.

GALEN (*c*.AD 200)

It was a cold, damp, spring day. A trio of earnest, gangling undergraduates came round the bend of the Iffley Road running track in Oxford, their feet crunching on the cinders at a speed that had only been wished for before. The tallest of the three took over the lead from his pacemakers and quickened his stride. Moments later, Roger Bannister became the first man on earth to run a mile in under 4 minutes. Since the clock had been accurate enough to measure the mile, men had been trying to achieve the impossible; now Bannister had done it. The date was 1954. Surely a man could not run much faster?

The following year, at the White City stadium in London, the first *three* runners, in what became known as 'The Mile of the Century', beat the 4 minute mark. Thirty-one years later, when Steve Cram set the current world record, he slashed nearly 13 seconds off Bannister's time. In a mythical contest between them, Bannister wouldn't even be in the home straight by the time Cram breasted the tape.

But a lot of things were different then. Chris Chataway was one of the pacemakers in Roger Bannister's first 4 minute mile, and beat the 4 minutes himself at White City and set numerous other records; he later became an MP and a

Front page story, all around the world; Roger Bannister achieves the impossible – a mile in under 4 minutes

Cabinet minister. 'International athletics does require a great deal of regular training,' he wrote then, 'I find that an hour at least must be sacrificed on most days of the week. It is important to train properly for a competition ... before an all-out effort an absolute minimum of training should be 2 or 3 days of running a week in the 3 weeks beforehand.'

That was an article for boys, in a British annual called *The Boys Book of all Sports* and no doubt Chataway was trying not to put young people off the sport. But his schedule was that of the old gifted amateur, who had other roles and interests in his life. He advised boys to treat the sport as a 'game'. In a few short years, the new disciplines of coaches like Arthur Lydiard and Percy Cerutty, and the greater seriousness in sport at the top, would make much heavier demands on athletes' bodies and commitment and shift track and field towards today's full time, dedicated, professional approach.

By the 1970s training for Seb Coe and his rivals had moved on more like a light year than a generation, matching the increased competitiveness in sport; that in turn has been part of the developing media attention and commercialism. All are part of the same equation. Sport has become tougher, as the rewards of winning have increased. Those rewards mean that the best athletes do not have to combine sporting effort with another career, as Chataway, Bannister, Emil Zatopek and the rest still had to do in the 1950s; but it also means that careers last longer.

Some records also last. Pietro Mennea's 200 metres world record set in 1979 remains unbeaten. Bob Beamon's Olympic long jump record in the rarefied air of Mexico in 1968 was not beaten until 1991, which was also the tenth anniversary of Sebastian Coe's famous 800 metres world record set in Florence. Looking back now Coe recalls 'The conditions were not as perfect as when I first broke the record in Oslo in 1979. This time it was late in the evening, mainly because the Italian time keeping had been slack. The race was more than an hour later than scheduled.' At a more northerly latitude, it might have become too cold to run quickly, but at midnight Florence

54

So high, so long to the rest. America's Bob Beamon takes the gold medal at the Mexico Olympics in 1968, with a leap that stayed in the record books for 23 years

in June was still warm. 'It may sound arrogant,' he said, 'but I knew at that stage of my career that when fully fit I was the fastest around over two laps. That night it was me against the clock. I ran just about as quickly as I could – it was my

55

maximum, controlled effort. I always felt that in the next couple of years I would improve the time, but they were years when I kept having either illness or injury.' So far no one has improved the time; the record is still there, tantalising the best middle distance runners each year. The man who has come closest to the record, Joachim Cruz of Brazil, underlines the sacrifices required: 'You can't train the way I do and go out with girls!'

But records are only part of sport, of any kind or at any level. Winning is the usual goal. At its flowing and fighting best, sport is an intense concentration of physical and mental ability. The heat of competition requires both; the human body is the ultimate machine for sport, but it needs the brain as the supreme computer. Jim Wohlford, the Milwaukee Brewers outfielder, said '90 per cent of baseball is half mental!' And Brendan Foster, the European 5000 metres champion in 1974 and now a commentator, put it this way: 'Winning is simply concentration, application and confidence.'

Golf champion Jack Nicklaus has all of these. He plays each shot in his mind: 'I never hit a shot even in practice without having a very sharp, in-focus picture of it in my head. It's like a colour movie. First I "see" the ball where I want to finish. Then the scene quickly changes and I "see" the ball going there. Then there's a sort of fade-out, and the next scene shows me making the kind of swing that will turn the previous images into reality.' Would that we all had that vision!

Mental strength can be trained and fostered, if not yet with the same precision as coach and athlete can enhance leg speed for example. Modern coaches have come to place proper emphasis on its importance in the making of winners. In 1991, for example, the England rugby union team used 'mental tapes' developed by Britain's National Coaching Foundation. The tapes cover concentration, goal setting, anxiety control and so on. It may be no coincidence that the England team broke a 28-year hoodoo by beating the Welsh on their home ground of Cardiff Arms Park in that year.

No doubt there will be more emphasis on mental training in sport's future. But less is known about the human mind than about the body. The science of physical fitness is now well developed. There is not yet the mental equivalent, for a coach, of prescribing 100 metre repetitions to build up finishing speed, or a specific weight training regime to develop upper body strength. Nevertheless, the sports psychologist is already an accepted member of coaching teams in some professional sports like American football and soccer.

Medicine helps the modern athlete too. Vastly better techniques and treatments are available. Quite slight injuries, which might have taken months to heal with water treatment and massage are eased in days or even hours with electrotherapy, ultrasound and lasers. Injuries that halted careers in the past are now being mended. In last year's English FA Cup Final, for example, the multi-million player Paul Gascoigne, of Tottenham Hotspur FC, was carried off with a torn cruciate ligament in the right knee. An operation was carried out the following day and the expectations of his full recovery were such that the Italian club Lazio went ahead with their proposed multi-million pound transfer. Ironically, the manager of the other team (Nottingham Forest FC) in the match, Brian Clough, suffered the same injury himself in 1958 when he was a star player and he never played again.

Medicine also affects diet. Dr Robert Voy, a former chief officer to the USOC (United States Olympic Committee) and the author of a book called *Drugs, Sport and Politics*, recorded one 'national track star's' diet as follows: 'Vitamin A, 1600 mg; B-complex capsules, 4 times a day; vitamin C, 200 mg; vitamin B6, 150 mg; calcium tablets, 4 daily; magnesium tablets, twice a day; zinc tablets, 3 per day; royal jelly capsules; garlic tablets; cayenne tablets; eight aminos; Gamma-Oryzanol; Mega Vit Pack; supercharge herbs; Dibencozide; glandular tissue complex; natural steroid complex; Inosine, Orchic testicle extract; Pyridium; Ampicillin; and hair rejuvenation formula with Biotin.' Voy says, 'and that was what he ADMITTED to taking!'

57

Reflections on mortality. The
funeral in Nottinghamshire of
cyclist Tommy Simpson.
Simpson collapsed and died
during the 1967 Tour de France
from an overdose of drugs

There is, of course, the dark side of science. In 1967 the great British cyclist, Tommy Simpson, the world champion two years earlier, was struggling up Mount Ventoux on the thirteenth day of the Tour de France. Suddenly, he was seen to lose control; his bike wobbled, he fell off. Frantic efforts were made to revive him, but he never recovered consciousness; a later autopsy revealed a mixture of high levels of methylamphetamine, amphetamine and cognac in his body. He was neither the first nor the last to die of the misuse of drugs; people pop pills, as well as pump iron, to gain that crucial advantage or edge all competitors seek. In 1974 Howard Payne, the British hammer thrower, said 'There are only two alternatives to taking anabolic steroids – don't take them and be second class, or give up athletics.'

Throughout time, the challenge of sport has led some to bend or break the rules in search of success. Greek athletes at the original Olympic Games developed various herb and food diets to help their performance; long distance runners favoured all-meat schedules, while the sprinters worked on dried figs!

Pat Connolly, American coach and critic of drug use, with one of her young charges, Randy Givens (left)

A modern 'Charter for Cheats' has been written in the laboratory, where performance enhancing drugs were developed. Sport was (usually) not their original purpose; most have important and legitimate uses in medicine. But particular drugs have been adapted to sporting competition, because they have properties which help athletes and players develop their bodies and their potential quicker and better, or both. Steroids enable athletes to extend the natural range of their physical fitness and strength, adding bulk and muscle strength and permitting longer and harder periods of training. Amphetamines can directly enhance performance, either in speed or stamina. Betablockers steady the nerves and hands of shooters and snooker players. On top of all of these are masking agents, to disguise the use of all of them!

In sport, all such drugs have a twisted purpose. Their object is not to reduce pain, or aid recovery from injury. They are an illicit means of gain; they enhance performance falsely and are thus contrary to the ethic of free and equal competition. Taking drugs is the same as any other form of cheating – done to gain advantage, unseen and undetectable to others.

Pat Connolly was a formidable American athlete, but is better known as coach to the legendary sprinter Evelyn Ashford. She's been involved in top women's athletics, as competitor and coach, for over 20 years. Connolly told us: 'People want to win, and drugs are a short cut. Once you're an Olympic champion your life is totally different. Opportunities come that you would not otherwise have had. And 1980s society is full of greed and getting ahead. It's just win at all costs.' She added: 'But I couldn't possibly go to an athlete and say you need to take drugs because, for me that would be telling them I don't believe in you.'

There have been siren voices in favour of a free market for drugs. From within and without sport, some have argued that using drugs to aid performance is just the same as benefiting from other technological advances in equipment, clothing, facilities and so on. They say that Jesse Owens won his races and records in the 1930s without starting blocks, tartan tracks,

59

efficient shoes and modern training techniques. Seb Coe made use of all those aids to performance and also consulted biochemists, physiologists, and orthotic experts.

Let Seb reply: 'First, all those modern developments are within the rules and they are there to be seen and checked, and all are available to other top athletes. Nothing secret or underhand is involved. Secondly, drugs do damage – they are a million miles from the healthy sport we all joined. We encourage young people to take up sport because it is good for them, physically and mentally; we think it is good for character development. The last thing we should do is bring them into something with the potential danger that drugs carry.'

Who is to say how long that argument will hold sway; even now it seems that sometimes it is held 'more in the breach than in the observance'. Drugs are outlawed and their use is sternly condemned by all the main sporting bodies and their leaders; but somehow the feeling persists that drug use and abuse is far more widespread in sport than the statistics of offences and offenders would indicate.

Early on in the drugs story, after the Tommy Simpson episode, for example, a real problem was the absence of effective detection methods. Professional cyclists used large doses of caffeine as a stimulant in the 1940s, 50s and 60s; boxers in the Olympic Games in 1960 took Varidase to minimise the effects of bruising. Steve Courson, formerly a NFL (America's National Football League) player with the Pittsburgh Steelers, told us that 'in the NFL in the early 60s amphetamine use was very open. Certain locker rooms had a cookie jar full of amphetamines where (players) could reach in and grab what they wanted. Steroid use started through the training room. One coach started giving his players Dianabol, an oral anabolic steroid, in 1963. It was placed in a little cup on the training table next to players' plates; the players weren't told what they were taking.'

Dr Robert Kerr, a former advisor to a number of Olympic athletes, has admitted giving performance enhancing drugs to athletes in the United States including 20 or more medal winners at the Los Angeles Olympic Games. He first encountered the practice as a rugby player: 'At the local gym I noticed how easily ... black market ... drugs that would enhance strength and speed were obtainable; it went against all the principles of being a physician as far as I was concerned.' Because many were 'fake medications' Dr Kerr decided to help athletes 'by evaluating and monitoring them both physically and with laboratory controls' and then giving them 'the right prescriptions for these drugs'. He hoped that the athletes would take advice and follow 'a much smaller regimen than they would on their own'. But Kerr found that many of his 'patients' simply supplemented what he provided from the black market he so disliked. He told us he was guilty of 'wishful thinking'. Dr Kerr says he gave up the practice in 1985 when twice in one day he found that patients had ignored his advice and taken larger doses of drugs than he had prescribed.

By the early 1970s performance enhancing drugs had apparently become almost the norm in many sports, in the continued absence of effective detection. The AMA (American Medical Association) estimated that amphetamines could improve runners' performances by 1.5 per cent and swimmers' by 1 per cent. Although the IOC (International Olympic Committee) had passed a resolution condemning what was now called 'doping' in 1962, it was 1969 before Professor Raymond Brooks at St Thomas' Hospital in London developed techniques for detecting the use of a range of drugs. At last, sports bodies had the weapons to fight a war, but the drugs have remained in use ever since. Why?

Two of the authors of this book have sifted through the evidence of drug use before. 'The Misuse of Drugs in Sport' report was written by Sebastian Coe, and the then Minister for Sport, Colin Moynihan MP, in 1987. David Teasdale was a Director at the Sports Council and helped in the analysis and drafting of the report.

During the writing of the report, checks were made on the arrangements at a particular athletics meeting at London's

Crystal Palace stadium, and significant flaws were found in the procedures. Some days before the meeting, for example, the testing lab at Chelsea College had actually received a list of the 'lanes and places' to be tested on the Sunday. The rules state that such a list should only be drawn up by the IAAF (International Amateur Athletics Federation) observer on the day of competition. The report team could not isolate a culprit, but clearly this was not a tight and secure system.

For this book we have examined further evidence and talked to people prepared to discuss their experience and what they have to say is both vivid and instructive.

Dr Robert Voy says that detection was largely ineffective before 1983, when gas chromotography and mass spectrometry was introduced. Dr Voy noted the significance of the 1983 Pan American Games, from which a number of leading US athletes withdrew just before the opening. Some arrived at Caracas, but then turned back. 'The information that they received was that the drug testing for the first time in history was to be so accurate as to diagnose the use of anabolic steroids and other drugs. ... Certain athletes chose to leave – rather than be tested.' Dr Voy believed that many of them were innocent, but 'a lot of athletes didn't trust drug testing; it was something new ... they didn't want to be subject to something they weren't sure they could trust.' Despite these departures, no fewer than 21 medal winners were tested positive and disqualified!

Just before the Pan American Games, the World Championships had taken place at Helsinki; here none of the tests on the medal winners proved positive. Dr Voy told us 'Many of the athletes claimed on leaving Helsinki that there had to be positives ... the rumour about was that there definitely were but they were not reported.'

Since drugs could be traced, and positives were now being found, sport was caught in a dilemma. Should it crack down on drug abuse, using the methods available, and clean up the sport? Or should it attempt to sweep the problem under the carpet, hoping it would get better, and thus not run the risk of frightening away the badly needed TV and sponsors with cries of 'unclean'?

Dr Charles Yesalis, Professor of Health and Human Development at Penn State University, sees the administrators' problem clearly: 'If sport was really cleaned up effectively, the number of national records being set would drop drastically and that ... sells sport around the world ... The public pay to see events, see athletics; they want to see bigger than life; they want to see records broken.' Pat Connolly sees it the same way: 'The authorities are in the business of making money. They're promoting a sport; they want to sell tickets; they want to sell TV time; they want to sell commercial sponsorship. And they can't do that if there's this image that athletes are not the clean, ideal people that the world would like to perceive them as.'

Sometimes simple observation should tell all. For example, physical changes have been noted in particular sportsmen and women that would have been unlikely to have occurred naturally. Steve Courson pointed out that NFL coaches might just as well write an anabolic steroid prescription when they advise players to 'gain 25 to 30 lbs and we think you'll be a starter next year'. Twenty-five pounds of muscle takes longer than that to develop without using steroids. 'How many men have you ever met,' Dr Robert Kerr asks rhetorically, 'who weighed 280 lbs who have a fairly narrow waist and who are as quick as the devil and can run as fast as can be? I don't believe I've ever met anyone like that. But you'll see a whole lot of them every time you watch an NFL football game.'

Perhaps women have been the most obvious ones to spot. Pat Connolly says: 'After working so hard for so many years and then watching the Eastern European athletes up close, we suspected they were using drugs, although not knowing them as kids we couldn't see the changes; but we could sort of dismiss it and say, well, we're better than they are. But, when the American women started using drugs we could see them change. We could hear their voices deepen, we could see the beard appear on their faces and their muscle definition

63

completely change. We could see them going from mediocre, weak athletes to these incredibly powerful, gifted super athletes, and I'm talking about women.' Connolly testified to the 1984 US Senate Biden Committee that she thought 15 of the 50 women on the American track and field team used steroids. Four years later she believed the number had increased.

Rightly, sports people cannot be pilloried on rumour; the only sure way of conviction lies in the firm evidence based on testing and detection. The Coe/Moynihan 1987 report highlighted the need to ensure that all testing regimes were independent and random – and that testing was frequent. As in any area of human transgression, the risk of being caught has to be sufficiently high to affect the plans and instincts of the potential transgressors; to make them think twice, before taking substances that may endanger their health as well as devalue their sporting efforts. There has to be a certainty that the testing cycle and procedure cannot be manipulated by the athletes, or their representatives, or by the governing bodies or administrators themselves. Sadly, we believe this is not yet the case – in attitude or practice.

In 1981, the American discus thrower Ben Plunknett was tested positive in Europe, but voted American Athlete of the Year at the end of the season.

Weaknesses in the testing system are illustrated by the case of the American, Butch Reynolds, current world record holder for 400 metres. On 12 August 1990 he was tested positive for the anabolic steroid, nandrolone, after a meeting in Monte Carlo. When the second (B) sample confirmed the finding he was suspended by the IAAF for two years.

Reynolds took his case to an American court which ruled that he was still eligible to appear in the United States national trials in June 1991. The Athletics Congress (TAC) accepted the ruling and allowed Reynolds to run, putting themselves in direct confrontation with the IAAF.

Fortunately for both, Reynolds finished seventh in his heat and thus failed to qualify for the World Championships in

64

Water, water everywhere, nor any time to think: Francois Cirotteau of France in a record kayak jump of 28 metres at Parc D'Ordesa in Spain (*Laurent Chevallier/Agence Vandystadt/Allsport, France*)

(*Above*) Croquet concentration at
Hurlingham
(*Adrian Murrell/Allsport*)

(*Right*) Out with the boys: Norway's Ingrid
Kristiansen with her pacemakers before her
fourth victory in the London Marathon in
1988 (*Allsport*)

(*Far right*) Gone with the wind: *America 3*
in the 1991 World Championships,
America's Cup Class
(*Mike Powell/Allsport*)

(*Above*) Over the top: New Zealand play Wales in the Women's Rugby World Cup, 1991. But women's rugby needs more television coverage and more sponsors
(*Dan Smith/Allsport*)

(*Left*) 'Twixt corn and sunflowers, riders in the 1991 Tour de France
(*Agence Vandystadt/Allsport, France*)

(*Overleaf*) Superstrider: America's Ed Moses, Olympic and world champion
(*Tony Duffy/Allsport*)

Flying high: Britain's Daley Thompson, in one of the ten decathlon disciplines, the pole-vault, at the Seoul Olympics (*Steve Powell/Allsport*)

The American 400 metres world record holder, Butch Reynolds, was tested positive for drugs in 1990

Tokyo in August that year. Meanwhile a three man panel from the TAC looked into Reynolds' case and in October cleared him of the drug charge. They maintained that the chain of custody procedure for handling the urine samples after the Monte Carlo meeting had been improperly followed and that the A and B phials tested by the IOC accredited laboratory in Paris were not from the same athlete. Put another way, as one of the Reynolds team insisted, someone was trying to 'fix' Butch Reynolds.

The LaFarge Laboratory in Paris was outraged. The IAAF, not the laboratory, were responsible for the transit of the samples, they insisted; as far as the test procedure was concerned it had been carried out according to normal practice. Two samples are always taken (to guard against errors) and both contained traces of nandrolone and both came from the same source. That source was Reynolds.

The case was referred to the IAAF for arbitration and at the time of going to press their judgment had not been delivered. In the wings lurks the threat of Reynolds' million dollar lawsuit against the TAC for loss of earnings; and this in a sport whose full council, meeting in Tokyo in August 1991, had voted to retain the word 'Amateur' in their title, the International Amateur Athletics Federation. But then, as Humpty Dumpty said in Lewis Carroll's *Alice Through the Looking Glass*: 'When I choose a word it means just what I choose it to mean – neither more nor less.'

When the Olympic Games were awarded to Los Angeles for 1984, there was not a single IOC accredited testing lab in the United States. Dr Voy says that the USOC's experience at the 1983 Pan American Games enabled them to 'put together the first real drug testing regime in the United States', but he admits that the pre-testing system (called an 'education programme') introduced before the 1984 Games had the effect of helping athletes learn how not to get caught.

Suspicion became fact in 1988. At the Games in Seoul, Ben Johnson had been acclaimed the world's fastest man for winning the 100 metres. A few hours later, he was the world's most disgraced. Tested positive, he tried to protest his innocence, but not for long. He left the heights of Olympism and the world's headlines in Seoul for his adopted home in Canada, his crime soon to be the subject of a major inquiry by the Canadian government under the Honourable Charles L. Dubin, Chief Justice of Ontario.

Johnson's coach, Charley Francis, in his book *Speed Trap*, described getting the news as 'the ultimate horror … like a fatal car crash; you knew it could happen at any time but you never believed it could happen to you.' Suddenly, the sports world had changed; this was overnight sensation. The cynics

On 24 September 1988 Ben Johnson became the world's fastest man, 100 metres in 9.79 seconds at the Seoul Olympics. Hours later he was disqualified after a positive drugs test

October 1988: Johnson denies using any drugs at a press conference, but his face told a different story. Later, he confessed to the Dubin Inquiry

66

would say that the sensation and the change was simply that Johnson got caught. His coach argues in his book that 'drugs are not banned because they are unethical, they are unethical because they are banned.' Dr Yesalis says, 'They caught him one time out of twenty; if I only did my job correctly one time out of twenty I wouldn't have a job right now.' Pat Connolly felt only disappointment and despair: 'I lost hope completely. I just said, it can't be done any more.' But she meant that the women culprits were not being caught, and announced her decision to get out of the sport.

In Canada, the Dubin Inquiry uncovered a network of drug taking in Canadian sport. It lasted 10 months and heard 119 witnesses; its report was released in June 1990. Before the Johnson affair, few people would have pointed even the finger of suspicion at Canada and its athletes. It was not a major nation in track and field; Johnson was indeed the only well-known competitor. But the Inquiry found that over 40 of its athletes were using drugs as part of their training and preparation. Robert Armstrong QC, Chief Counsel to the Inquiry, said that 'we lost our innocence as a sporting nation in Seoul.' The question has to be asked, however, if there were 40 and maybe even more in a country like Canada, how many drug users were there in successful track and field teams like the British and American?

Charley Francis, who was heavily criticised by the Dubin Inquiry and sacked as a coach, has claimed that drug use among top track and field stars has been widespread for a number of years. As a coach, he said, he had to recommend drugs to help his charges keep up with everyone else! He can offer no proof; and the libel laws have prevented his naming names. But the Francis voice will continue to nag the conscience of world sport: 'If every coach and athlete told the truth about drug use, it would force a public re-evaluation of sport.'

Some heartening evidence does exist of the impact of effective rules and systems. Some athletes of dubious build have slipped from the scene in recent years. One can only be cynical about some of these 'retirements'. More certainly, perhaps, the recent fall in standards in some events – notably, in track and field – graphically illustrates the extent of drug taking and its impact on performance. The chart below plots the 'progress' in three events.

Women's 1500	1982	1988	1991
Fastest	3:54.23	3:53.96	3:59.16
10th fastest performer	3:59.24	4:01.02	4:05.04
Number of sub-4:00 performers	11	2	1
Women's 3000	1982	1988	1991
Fastest	8:26.78	8:26.53	8:32.00
10th fastest	8:36.54	8:37.70	8:42.02
Number of sub-8:35 performers	6	7	1
Men's Shot	1984	1988	1991
Longest	22.19	23.06	22.03
10th longest	21.63	21.16	20.41
Numbers of 21 metres + puts	22	15	1

The athletes themselves know what has happened. Wendy Sly, the British athlete who won a silver medal in Los Angeles in 1984, told us: 'in 1988 I was ranked tenth in the world at 3000 metres, but today that time would get me in the top four. The difference is drugs, and the hold they've had on the sport'.

The change in Russian domestic rules in 1989 which made the taking of drugs in sport liable to severe penalties (a possible 2-year ban for the first offence, and a life-time ban for the second) reduced that country's team in the 'strong' disciplines from world élite to average levels.

But the case study of drug abuse must lie in what was East Germany. That country decided in the late 1960s that sport could provide an easy and cheap route to the national prestige its leaders coveted. In particular, their sports administrators targeted some 'soft' events, notably, in women's track and field. The results achieved over the next 20 years were nothing short of remarkable. A small country of the size of Ireland came to dominate sections of world athletics, producing dozens of World and European champions and record holders, and Olympic medallists.

Pat Connolly noted a calculation in their cheating: 'In the USA every athlete was on their own; if they wanted to cheat they had ... to get the stuff themselves. These East Germans didn't even necessarily have to know they were even taking drugs. They were just given them because there was a methodology that fitted right in hand with their political philosophy.'

In November 1990 the German magazine *Stern* published what they said were detailed East German team documents illustrating a planned programme of drug use involving many famous names. These included Kristin Otto (the world champion swimmer who won six gold medals in Seoul), Heike Drechsler (gold medallist and world record holder in sprints and long jump), Ulf Timmerman (world record holder in the shot put), Jurgen Schult (Seoul discus gold medallist), Christian Schenk (decathlon gold medal in Seoul). The magazine reported 'a complete, methodical and almost meticulous picture of drug usage.' It was all co-ordinated by the Research Institute for Body Culture and Sport (in Leipzig) and the Medical Sports Association. The drugs centre was within the Association building in East Berlin. Dr Manfred Hoppner, the director of the competitive sport section, told *Stern*: 'We used anabolic steroids strictly according to medical considerations. The state of well-being of the athlete was meticulously analysed and ... checked ... According to my knowledge no country in the world has treated its athletes better, even after the end of their careers.' The starting point was the Montreal Olympics: 'We knew what the Americans were doing – and we wanted to stay in competition.'

A year later, in 1991, *The Times* reported that a West German molecular biologist had uncovered secret East German documents showing that the doping of athletes to

She's moved from East to West, but Heike Drechsler stands accused of taking drugs under the old regime

improve their performance was a State sponsored plan costing millions of Marks. East German scientists had even gained doctorates for their work on steroids and other illegal drugs in sport.

The East Germans had an IOC accredited drug testing laboratory at Kreischa, near Dresden, whose head was Dr Claus Clausnitzer; and he was a member of the Drugs Sub-Committee of the IAAF and the IOC's medical commission – the two crucial committees responsible for the fight against drug abuse in track and field around the world.

Pat Connolly spotlighted another issue, that women can get results from smaller doses of drugs, which are therefore more difficult to detect: 'I can take testosterone today and pass the test tomorrow. No officials are addressing the issue of women and drugs.' The East German women have gone, but their dominance could be repeated by a country or group prepared to risk flouting the rules.

Charles Dubin concluded the inquiry in 1988 saying: 'I am convinced that the problem is widespread not only in Canada but also around the world. The evidence shows that banned ... substances and in particular anabolic steroids are being used by athletes in almost every sport, most extensively in weightlifting and in track and field.'

Why, then, are so few offenders caught? Firstly, we know that detection methods are not yet good enough. Park Jong Sei, the test director at the Seoul Olympics, claimed that he and his team 'could find a thimbleful of a banned substance in a swimming pool,' but Arne Ljungquist, Vice President of the IAAF and Chairman of its Medical Committee, says, 'there are many, many more substances for which it is not possible to test.' Charley Francis reports that he was 'spinning with confusion' on his way to discuss the Johnson positive with the IOC testers because the sprinter had been using the steroid furazabol and 'I knew that it couldn't be detected, since the IOC's lab equipment hadn't been programmed to identify furazabol ...'

Secondly, testing arrangements are not yet sufficiently

effective. Dr Charles Yesalis of Penn State describes them as a farce: 'I've seen no indications over the last two decades that the level of drug use has stopped, in fact I think it's increased. Testing has caused athletes to switch from one drug to another, or change their dose. It's just too simple to beat.'

Even if tests are being done for the right substances, they are being done at the wrong time. For too long the emphasis has remained on testing in competition, although it is well known that athletes could make sure that substances were out of their bodies in time. As Dr Voy put it: 'Someone is told on December 11 that on January 11 a policeman will be waiting at the end of his driveway to inspect his driver's licence ... only a fool would not have things in order when he runs into the policeman.' Sir Arthur Gold, Chairman of the BOA (British Olympic Association) and a leading international anti-drug campaigner, echoes this view: 'only the foolish and the ill advised get caught.'

At the Dubin Inquiry, an exasperated Robert Armstrong concluded, after a lengthy cross-examination of IAAF and other witnesses, that 'the last 16 years of in-competition testing had been largely a waste of time and money.'

The answer is regular and frequent out-of-competition testing, as the Coe/Moynihan Report recommended, and as the IAAF has now decreed. But this has to be effectively monitored too. The Canadian Track and Field Association decided in 1982 on a policy of out-of-competition testing, but the first tests were carried out only after Seoul. In the wake of Seoul and the Johnson case, the USOC adopted such a programme to be implemented by The Athletics Commission (TAC). But, saying they were short of trained people, the TAC cut the programme from 52 weeks to 13 and exempted any athlete who lived or trained more than 75 miles from the nearest testing site. Of the 294 athletes called for tests, 175 were excused on these grounds!

The Dubin inquiry criticised both the IAAF and the IOC on this issue. The Chief Justice noted that: 'despite knowing the fallacy of in-competition testing, as they have for many years, (they) have taken no steps to make the fallacy more widely known.'

There is a third reason for the continuing use of drugs in sport and it is the most serious of all. Is there malpractice in governing bodies, domestic and international?

Dr Voy is in little doubt of this. He's expressed his concern about the manipulation of test arrangements in the USA and at international events. He says, for example, that: 'The legal rights of the cheaters have, in my mind, sometimes been used as smoke screens to hide behind ... it is a money game and they protected the ones who brought back the medals.' When he worked with TAC on the mid-80s test programme: 'it soon became obvious that the big name athletes knew damn well what events to stay out of and when. Somebody had to have been tipping the athletes off.'

No less an athlete than Daley Thompson is in no doubt, either: 'They've all turned a blind eye. Their feeling is, if we

A new generation, a new start, but can they win without drugs?

haven't caught any, we haven't got any. Why? Because it means more TV, more money, more trips for the boys.'

Robert Armstrong, Chief Counsel to the Dubin inquiry, said in an address to an international symposium in Monte Carlo in February 1991 that: 'Many of these organisations (national and international) have been not much more than indifferent to the fight against drugs in sport.' The Dubin report itself had said: 'It is unfortunate that (the IAAF) has not used its influence in a more meaningful way to eradicate the drug problem ... (its) posture appears to have been to react to the problem only after the fact.' It also expressed 'concern that the IAAF appears to have made no investigation of very serious allegations made public in other inquiries.'

How can sport change the course of the game? The answer lies with leadership. If the governing bodies mean what they frequently say about the evils of drugs, they must ensure that the right systems are in place to detect and deter their use. In the words of NFL player Steve Courson: 'as a society we have been very unwilling, or maybe unable, to deal with our addiction to sports and winning.' The international federations of sport and the administrators, with the full support of participants at all levels, must deal effectively with that addiction.

The leaders must resolve their conflicts of interest. As Dr Voy observes, too often 'the fox looks after the henhouse'. Testing must be entirely independent of national and international sports bodies, unaffected by their preoccupation with medals and money. There has to be proper accountability.

The responsibility of leadership, in every sports body, is to ensure the future health of the sport and its participants. There must be no more Ben Johnsons – either in first or second or any other place in sport. The fact that he was not alone does not excuse him, as his coach has argued, nor indeed does it excuse his advisers, his governing body and others. Sport's task now is to sweep away suspicion; and the carpet. It must tackle what Robert Armstrong QC called 'the decline of ethical values which pervade modern day sporting competition.'

73

5 My kingdom for a horse

A horse! A horse! My kingdom for a horse!

KING RICHARD AFTER THE BATTLE OF BOSWORTH,
IN SHAKESPEARE'S *RICHARD III*

Charles Dickens once observed that there is 'a passion for hunting, something deeply implanted in the human breast.' He was right; hunting is rooted in our pre-history where it commands a mystical status which transcends our ancestors' need for food. In the Dordogne, in France, in caves hidden from man for thousands of years, are found some of the earliest examples of man's artistic expression. Dating from about 20 000 BC, most of the illustrations are of animals and most of the contexts are hunting scenes. Human beings are rarely depicted and when they are, it is without the astonishing accuracy and detail of the animals.

Detailed studies of the ancient cave paintings have led to a consensus view that the pictures, quite apart from their extraordinary artistic merit, had considerable symbolic significance. That the hunt became an important mystical ritual is hardly surprising, since hunting was central to survival. But it also seems from the pictures that hunting already had a sporting element.

These early paintings also provide evidence of animal sacrifice. Such ceremonies celebrated success in the hunt and reinforced the power of the hunters over the animals. And it is these rituals designed to signify power over animals that serve as the earliest representation of athletic performance.

The Palio – Italy's most famous horse race, run every year around the magnificent medieval square in Sienna

75

Strategies for hunting were planned in advance. Rehearsals and practice sessions would have formed an important part of the daily routine. It is easy to imagine contests among the hunters for the accolade of 'strongest', 'quickest', 'bravest' and so on. Success in the hunt must have been reflected in the social prowess of the very early hunter. It is hardly surprising that the best hunters became leaders and as societies developed, those leaders became kings. Prowess in hunting and skill with weapons became synomymous with the power of kingship. Sadly perhaps, the areas of the world where societies can hunt for food has shrunk almost to nothing. Nowadays, in the developed world, hunting is a sport, and a controversial one.

As in the earliest days, the horse remains our constant and reliable companion, in the hunt and in many other sports. Shakespeare's Richard III would have traded in his kingdom for a horse. For centuries gamblers around the world have echoed the sentiment, and collectively lost fortunes as well as shirts. What started as a chase became a race and we have since raced horses, dogs, ostriches, frogs, pigeons, and all manner of other beasts. But the horse remains the most popular and the most valuable. On a horse – its pace and/or its progeny – rest some of the biggest prizes in sport. The legend that bookmakers always win in the end does not deter millions from the fun of a bet, even those who have never actually seen a horse race! Horse racing is a major industry around the world; there is scarcely a country which does not boast a racing tradition of its own.

The horse is central in other sports too – in the ancient game of polo, or in show jumping and eventing, for example, and also features in bull fighting and rodeo. And the horse retains the link with the chase in what, in Britain at least, is probably the most controversial sport of all – fox hunting.

In Britain hunting followed warfare as the sport of kings. The phrase was probably introduced into the national psyche by two obscure English poets three hundred years ago; by way of an aside they are worth quoting. Sir William Davenant, a Poet Laureate in the mid-seventeenth century, wrote eloquently of war in 'The Soldier Going to the Field':

For I must go where lazy Peace
Will hide her drowsy head;
And, for the sport of kings, increase
The number of the dead.

A century later, William Somerville, in his one remembered poem, 'The Chase', wrote:

My hoarse-sounding horn
Invites thee to the chase, the sport of kings;
Image of war, without its guilt.

Since the Middle Ages, hunting had been the sport of kings because it had been the preserve of kings. Then they hunted deer, which the court chased on horseback with bows and arrows, for food and for sport. Nobody pretends to be hunting deer for food nowadays, at least not with horse and hound; deer hunting and its more common cousin, fox hunting, remain fiercely argued 'sports'. For most, but not all, of the horse riding fraternity, the number of foxes needs to be controlled and hunting to hounds is an effective, and humane, method of doing so – providing great sport along the way.

Certainly, riding to hounds can be marvellously exhilarating; but to say it is an 'image of war, *without its guilt*' is arguable beyond the pages of a book like this. 'When a man wantonly destroys one of the works of man, we call him a vandal. When he destroys one of the works of God, we call him a sportsman,' said the American essayist, Joseph Wood Krutch.

Even where animals are cast as partners, rather than prey, questions have been raised about their exploitation for gain, and about training methods. The normally placid world of show jumping plunged into controversy when a video was produced showing the champion German rider, Alwin Schockemöhle, 'rapping' his horses' legs during training to make them jump higher. The 1990 World Equestrian Games in Stockholm was thrown into chaos when sponsors withdrew their support. Subsequently Schockemöhle retired from the sport.

Some horses' delight in scaling fences in the show jumping ring is obvious; like their riders they can rise to the big occasion and appreciate the support of the crowd. And no one who has been atop a horse, galloping away with the desire to be first, would doubt the animal's joy in racing. But in any sport, high performance demands hard work in preparation and in competition. Although the racing fraternity would cite the love and care devoted to their charges, on which fortunes are won and lost, their sport relies on the whip hand and often the hard bit as well. Horse and rider are a team, but only one can talk – about their health or fitness, motivation and racing needs, or their condition on the day. (Though some athletic and football coaches might make the same complaint about their charges!)

Six feet off the ground! Annette Miller (née Lewis) of Great Britain riding Tutien in the international event at Hickstead in 1987

A unique feature of animal sports is that the subjects are actually bred for success. Modern day racing stock can be traced back in the direct male line to only three out of hundreds of Arabian, Turkish or Barbary steeds imported into England during the seventeenth and early eighteenth centuries. The Godolphin Arabian or Barb, the Darly Arabian, and the Byerley Turk provided the male blood line for the entire English thoroughbred racing stock, which in turn has provided the stock for American thoroughbreds. Now the breeding studs in Britain and Ireland, and in Kentucky in America, which dominate the racehorse markets, export their stock all over the world and command fabulous prices. The best yearlings at the Tattersalls High Flyer Sales, at New-market (for horses that have not yet raced, let alone won) may cost in excess of £1 million ($1.79 million). The value of a classic winner at stud today can be anything up to £10 million or more! Northern Dancer, the greatest stallion of the century, who died in 1990, sired 634 foals which were sold at public auction for a total of nearly £79 million ($184 million). Since 1791, there has been a *General Stud Book* compiled and published regularly in England (by Weatherby) which registers all thoroughbred horses throughout the world. Owners and agents plot successful 'matches' and invest. The process of foreplay and of copulation are conducted with industrial efficiency.

The origins of organised racing are lost in history but chariot racing is described in the *Iliad*, written some two and a half thousand years ago. Mounted horses were certainly raced in the Olympics in the sixth century BC.

Flavours of those ancient races survive today. In Italy, the historic Sienna Palio is still run twice a year in July and August around the magnificent medieval square in the centre of the city. The complex rules which have governed it since 1659 ensure that politics and ritual play their part as the 17 divisions of the city, or *contrade*, compete for glory.

Only ten of the *contrade*, selected on a rota system, can compete in any one Palio which is run in three laps of the 333 metre circumference of the Piazza del Campo. Although considered by some to be hard on the horses, it is almost certain that the impetus of tradition will ensure the survival of one of the world's best known races.

One of the first references to racing in Britain is in a

document by a secretary to Thomas à Becket, Archbishop of Canterbury, in the twelfth century who wrote that 'the jockeys, inspired with thoughts of applause, and in the hope of victory, clap spurs to the willing horses, brandish their whips and cheer them with their cries.' It could almost be Epsom Downs in the 1990s!

The earliest accounts are often of matches between two 'running horses', where one owner has wagered his steed against that of another. If they were knights, the test was

Big money on the nose. John Reid astride Tony Bin heading the field in the 1988 Prix de L'Arc de Triomphe at Longchamp in Paris. The richest race in Europe netted Tony Bin's owner almost half a million pounds in prize money

before the King and Court. In popular parlance today at any rate, racing has replaced hunting as the sport of kings because of the continued interest of the crowned heads of Europe and perhaps the British Royal Family in particular.

The first permanent racecourse with an annual fixture was established at Chester in 1540; the Newmarket Gold Cup was first run in 1634. Soon after that, King Charles II decreed that Newmarket should be the headquarters of horse racing. King Charles himself could never win the Gold Cup, but he did win the Plate on 14 October 1671. The Epsom Derby was not run until 1780, thirty years after the formation of The Jockey Club, which has been the ruling body of British racing ever since. By the time Queen Victoria came to the throne of Britain and its Empire in 1837, the sport of racing was very much as it is today. Except for women, who were not allowed to race until 1972!

Once bred, and sold, thoroughbreds still have to be trained into champions before their earning potential can be realised. In the old days, it might have been said that wagers were there to be won; today, the language is rather of investment needing to be recouped. For trainers around the globe today there is the ancient art of horsemanship and a new science of veterinary care and development. A mixture of both is necessary for real success.

For Henry Cecil, the famous keeper of the Warren Place training tradition at Newmarket, England, the training of a Classic racehorse is an art. Cecil has won numerous great international races, including three Epsom Derbies. He holds the record for the highest winnings in a flat racing season in 1987 (£1 896 689 ($3.1 million) from 180 winners). His stable jockey is the American Steve Cauthen, the only jockey to win Classic races on both US and European tracks. Their triumphs together have included Reference Point, which led the Epsom Derby from start to finish in 1987 and won the St Leger and King George VI and Queen Elizabeth II Diamond Stakes in the same year.

Touring his beautiful stables, one is made more aware of

81

an art gallery than a factory. Everything is superbly clean and equine masterpieces peer through the frame of each stable door. Cecil has over 160 horses in training at any one time, and he is nowhere happier than out on the gallops early in the morning on Newmarket Heath.

Henry Cecil is something of an eccentric, even old fashioned figure. Lean and mannered, he is often dressed in leggings and suede cowboy boots, all in blue, matching a tight-fitting sweater. His leisured manner conceals a tough determination to produce winning horses. Cecil told us that if it used to be the sport of kings 'now it's an industry, and a cut-throat one at that.' His approach may seem old fashioned to some. He has never used a stop-watch to time horses; he does not take a pulse; he eschews the scientific advances in performance measurement and encouragement that have been seized upon by other trainers and by other sports. 'You have to get horses there without them realising it,' he argues. 'You can't persuade them to go through a pain barrier – like you can with people. The best horses are often lazy in a gallop. It's important they don't hurt themselves. If their lungs are hurting, the next time they will resent it. It's important they give a performance first time out.'

Nicky Coe, the winner of the pre-eminent three day event, the Badminton Horse Trials, in 1990 (and ranked third in the world that year), told us that generally 'people who are working with animals in sport are doing so because they love them.' The feeling is obvious with Henry Cecil. Watching him go into a stall (with the 1990 Epsom Derby favourite, Razeen) was like seeing a penguin slide from land into water. But he talks unemotionally about horses, which he says have been abused for centuries, and about thoroughbreds in particular: 'They are a backward type of animal; they can probably only run two or three times at their peak.' He cited the 1989 Epsom Derby winner, Slip Anchor, as a perfect example which was at his best pace and performance only three times in his racing life. Cecil answers, in part, a question the authors of this book wanted to address. Why have humans run faster and faster and horses haven't? Why is it, for example, that the fastest time for the Derby at Epsom was set back in 1938 (by Mahmoud), since when all human racing records have been shattered and continue to be? The world mile record has been cut from 4.06 minutes to 3.46.

Firstly, Cecil believes that for generations, racehorses have been bred for pace, at the expense of strength, or, as he terms it, 'constitution'. He bemoans the loss some years ago of the sturdy German horse blood lines; the outcome is that modern racehorses cannot be worked too hard. As a result, some of the intensive, repetitive training methods successful in athletics cannot be adapted for horses. Secondly, thoroughbreds entered for the Classic races are young animals. Their flat racing career is over by the time they are four or five years old. In human equivalents, they are finished as infants. In Cecil's view they are too young for the tough methods of the coach in other sports. In addition, 'they only have a certain amount of petrol in the tank. It is easy to let two-year-olds do too much and then they disappoint in what should be their crucial third year.'

Cecil asked Seb Coe how much he would expect to 'blow' after a race. The response was not at all. For the top athlete the race day is a day off; the hard work is done in training when the mind and body are prepared and attuned for greater levels of exertion than should be necessary on the track. But the Cecil thoroughbred racehorses will only run the full race distance in the target race itself. A prize horse, scheduled for the two and a half mile Ascot Gold Cup, for instance, might have only ever raced one and a half miles beforehand.

There is of course some common ground. Cecil's winter training builds up stamina, as does the athlete's. Cecil aims to move from trot to canter to gallop as the season and the targets approach. And on the race day the respective champions may be spotted early and easily. The good track coach can pick the athlete readiest for the fray in a class track race. Henry Cecil can also see the champion in the parade ring. He or she is assessing the surroundings, and the opposition. The champion is 'the leader of the herd' and many a punter thinks it shows before the hooves hammer in earnest.

In training, both the champion horse or human can be deceptive. They can appear lazy, holding back their power and pace for the days that matter. The owner of Reference Point had a disappointing visit to see his horse with Henry Cecil the day before the 1987 Derby. Cecil recalls being very pleased with the colt and his performance that morning; he had actually worked a little harder than usual in the gallops. But he was still lagging behind others of more average pedigree and potential and the owner required a great deal of reassurance. The following day, with Steve Cauthen in the saddle Reference Point led from start to finish.

We went to Warren Place to discuss the science of horse racing with Henry Cecil; he convinced us it was an art. Cecil has the kind of skill and insight that has marked out the horseman since the earliest times. Perhaps the greatest English jockey, Lester Piggott, told us: 'Henry uses the old fashioned way, the traditional methods. But you can't take it away from him – he has the best average of winners and runners of all flat trainers.' Of course, even his art can fail sometimes. Cecil had a bad patch in 1991, the worst in the 23 years he has had a trainer's licence. He said then: 'My horses are under a cloud. There is something a little bit wrong and I am trying to eliminate it. I don't know if it's the oats, the hay or whatever. I am trying to change it round. The horses just don't seem to be firing and don't look right, and they come back looking dreadful. They have not got the virus. They have all been blood tested. But there is something wrong and I don't know what it is … I am doing exactly the same things as I have done for 22 years, so it is rather puzzling.'

Later in that season Cecil's results did improve. But experts the world over would sympathise with his predicament. For anyone involved in sport, ups and downs in form are expected; and coaching is all the harder with dumb animals.

The appliance of science should help; at any rate it seems

to for another, rather more controversial, British trainer. For Martin Pipe, the preparation of winning horses is very much a science. Pipe operates in the steeplechase market, called national hunt racing in Britain. He has broken many records in the last few years and became the first trainer ever to saddle over two hundred winners in one season in 1990.

Pipe's base in Somerset uses all the modern aids believed to benefit the racing (and jumping) horse. He takes temperatures and pulses twice a day; he monitors, scientifically, the physical condition of each of his horses; he has a swimming pool and an artificial track and various other training aids. In his no less immaculate stable yard you can see clearly an industry at work. Cecil regrets the needs and demands of industry, but Pipe enjoys and exploits them.

Some 30 years ago jockeys realised that, in part at least, their sport was a numbers game. The more they rode the more winners they had. Thus, the champion jockey was probably the one who had the most rides in a season. Martin Pipe has adopted the same logic and strategy, running his horses as often as possible. He sends horses to races of all classes, any-where in Britain. He plays the numbers game and he thus makes efficient sense of his industry, for his owners. His is a dream game. His owners usually have much less wealth than those in flat racing, but their motivation is the same – they want to win. They dream of seeing their horse come home first and then of leading him or her into the unsaddling enclosure. They pay a trainer to fulfil their dream for them.

Pipe's methods do not go uncriticised. Specifically, some have claimed that his wastage rates are significantly higher than any other major trainer; in other words fewer of his horses than average are fit enough to return to training the following year. Opponents have claimed that he is ruthless with his horses, that they are too much the products of a factory approach to winning. Some animals are thought to be pushed too hard. But many of Pipe's horses have already run and failed on the flat, so steeplechasing is their second career. He himself says that 'they already have a large mileage on

the clock when they come to me – so they will not last as long.'
Clearly, he could not achieve such levels of success without
exceptional skills of horsemanship. Lester Piggott is a strong
supporter. For him, Pipe is one of those 'that come along once
in a lifetime and does something different – and he has a
marvellous record'.

Piggott rode his first Derby winner, Never Say Die, in 1954.
Looking back now over his famous career, he notes a vast
number of changes – the photo finish, starting stalls, course
patrols, plastic instead of wooden railings, and so on. 'Race
tracks are better looked after and safer,' he told us. Like
Cecil, Piggott feels the sport is more of an industry now.
'Thoroughbreds have always been raced at 2 and 3 years old,
but up till the 1970s they used to train on for longer. Since
then, owners don't want to risk damage, or reduced value;
it's such an industry now, they can't afford the risk.' What
Piggott calls the 'money angle' is dominant, and the enthusiasts see less than they would like of the great horses like
Reference Point, Slip Anchor, Mill Reef and many more.

The game of polo probably even pre-dates racing, at least as
far as an organised event. The Persian poet Firdausi described
a match between the Persians and the Turkomans about 600
BC. There are the remains of an ancient polo ground at
Istaphan 300 yards long with stone goalposts 8 feet apart, the
same as today's measurements. Thousand-year-old Chinese
wall murals of the Tang Dynasty depict women playing polo
dressed in colourful, and voluminous dresses.

The name polo comes from the 'pulu', a willow root from
which the balls were made in Tibet. The Afghans played with
a goat's stomach, called a 'bushkazi'. The game spread over
Asia to Japan and China, and was discovered by the British
army in India in the nineteenth century, where it survives
today. One of the most thrilling sporting spectacles in the
world must be the annual polo tournament played on top of
the Shandur Pass in the Hindu Kush in Kashmir. A team
from Chitral take four days to ride to the pass to meet their

Chinese ladies were playing polo a thousand years ago, as this Tang Dynasty mural shows

opponents from Gilgit who've taken six days to get there – it's the only level ground between the two towns, and nearly 16 000 feet above sea level. Overlooking the highest polo ground in the world, the fabulous mountains of the Himalayas stretch heavenwards for another 10 000 feet or more.

Indian princes took up the game and they and the British army were its main supporters in India. Captain Joseph Sherer is credited with being the father of modern polo; he first organised the game in Assam in the 1850s. The first match in England was played at Hounslow in 1871 between the 9th Lancers and the 10th Hussars. The famous Hurlingham club was inaugurated soon after. The army has continued to be the chief supporter of the sport in England, as it was in India.

Polo was introduced to the USA in the 1870s by the publisher and newspaper magnate, Gordon Bennett, who was later to do so much for motor sport. By the time the First World War started, it had become well known, but most popular in countries with plenty of sun and horses – India, Argentina, South Africa and Spain. In these countries, as in England, polo has increasingly become the pastime of the armed services, or the very rich. In Britain the game has seen something of a revival in recent years because of the interest of Prince Charles. And for fans fortunate enough not to live too far away, a day's top polo perhaps offers better value for money than some other sports. A typical afternoon's programme might include two or three games featuring different teams.

To play though, requires considerable patronage, or wealth enough to keep a string of polo ponies. Normally a pony would not be ridden in more than two chukkas, and there can be eight to a game. The writer Rintoul Booth suggested that the animals are not a breed but a type, and not really ponies at all: 'Like polo players they can be of any size and are frequently well-bred, though you would never guess from the shocking language they use.'

The nineteenth-century sportswriter Robert Surtees suggested that there was 'no secret so close as that between a rider and his horse'. And it is in 'eventing' that perhaps the partnership between horse and human is seen most fully. Many argue that the greatest demands are made on horses in the three day event, or the 'Military' as it used to be called (it originated as a cavalry discipline). It has been an Olympic sport since 1912, initially with five events, only changing to its present form after the Second World War. Over three days, horse and rider undergo trials in dressage, cross country and finally show jumping. Champions require strength, stamina and agility and overall fitness of a high order. Nicky Coe says that the top horses can manage probably only nine or ten major events in their careers. Rarely can a rider pick up a horse just before an event and compete on it, as the top jockeys are used and expected to do in flat or jump racing. In the three days of competition, a team trust is needed between horse and rider and this is what competitors work to achieve. The bond developed between horse and rider in this event is much more akin to owner and pet. There is also a camaraderie about the sport which struck Seb Coe when he first became involved in eventing through his wife Nicky: 'When we walked the cross country course at Badminton, I was amazed at the free discussion between the competitors. They worked out together the safest and best line to take at the various jumps and obstacles. I could not imagine such an atmosphere in any other modern sport.'

However, eventing, like steeplechasing, can be tough for the horse. For Nicky Coe one big difference between these sports is that eventing fences have to be jumped over rather than pushed through. 'In the cross country at Badminton, when I won, I was going as fast as I would ever go in the final stages. But I was also making sure that there was enough petrol left to jump four or five difficult fences. And I had to make sure the horse would pass the following morning's vet inspection so we could enter the show jumping in the afternoon and complete the competition. The steeplechaser may not have to come out again for three weeks or more.' Therefore, on the day of the race they must be pushed harder, and usually are.

Horses jump naturally but they still require patient schooling to become top class whether as show jumpers, eventers, or steeplechasers. The writer Philip Walsh likened horse to children in that 'they'll learn something bad quicker than they'll learn something good'. The controversy surrounding Schockemöhle highlighted schooling techniques, but his use of 'rapping' was and is not unique. 'Rapping' describes the technique of catching a horse by its back or front shins (whichever is deemed to be the problem) as the animal clears a fence, to encourage it to jump higher. This can be done with a light aluminium pole placed a couple of inches above the top of the fence, perhaps triggered by a spring. Such a light pole will not hurt the horse; it is rather the noise that 'frightens' it to jump higher next time. But horses can be 'rapped' with a thicker pole, perhaps held by two people on either side of the fence who lift it sharply as the horse clears the obstacle. It is obvious that the practice of 'rapping' can be either kind or cruel, and either justifiable coaching or intimidation, according to the way it is done. However, Nicky Coe says 'a good jumper doesn't need rapping.'

89

There are plenty of other training methods that the unscrupulous will try, which give the lie to the view that success with animals is only possible with kindness. Trainers have been known to blister horses' legs, so that they are then very sensitive to any touch and so are likely to jump higher. Horses' 'boots', or leggings, can be made with studs on the inside, to achieve the same result. Such techniques are outlawed, but like illegal drugs, they are often hard to detect.

Any champion, however much they love their mount, needs to win to be the champion. The great jockey Lester Piggott has had few peers in horsemanship, but he has been found guilty of rough riding and he is by no means unique. One story though illustrates his champion's will to win. After losing his whip in a melee in mid-race, he seized a replacement from another jockey and went on to win; the subsequent steward's inquiry disqualified him. Piggott's only defence was his usual honest one: 'The other bloke wasn't going to win anyway.'

For the horse, the cruellest sport of all must be the bullfight. Indeed for Ernest Hemingway 'in the tragedy of the bullfight the horse is the comic character.' The horse at any rate is only a bit player, carrying the picador whose task is to plant garlanded spears into the neck muscles of the bull to slow it down and weaken its resistance. During the 'exchanges' the horse is often drugged and is protected only by padding and frequently ends up gored. 'The tragic climax of the horse's career,' wrote Hemingway in *Death in the Afternoon*, 'has occurred off-stage at an earlier time; when he was bought by the horse contractor for use in the bullring.' Many would argue that it is crueller still for the bull, which will end up dead, but supporters swear it is an even contest between man and beast. Bullfighting is steeped in ancient tradition and mysticism and for those in love with it any argument that it might not be a sport is acceptable only because they believe it to be an art. In Spain it is riven deep into the country's heritage and remains an important tourist attraction.

Between March and October 40 million people will go to the bullfight – 20 per cent of whom will be tourists. There are

Death in the afternoon. However 'glorious' the Corrida, horse deaths in bullfighting go unrecorded

90

between 300 and 400 *plazas de toros* in Spain, the largest, in Madrid, holding almost 24 000 spectators. Few, apparently can make a profit; most rely on grants from local councils. The best matadors can earn £8000 ($14 000) for one fight, and tickets to see them cost perhaps £180 ($320), twice the price of a good seat at the opera in Madrid.

A *corrida de toros* consists of the putting to death of six bulls in a public bullring in accordance with a defined ritual. The traditional time is five o'clock in the afternoon, after siesta, but when the sun is still burning. The best seats are definitely those with the sun behind them. The Spanish say *El sol es el mejor terero* – 'the sun is the best bullfighter'. For Hemingway, without the sun 'the best bullfighter is not there ... he is like a man without a shadow'.

As a spectacle, the bullfight has few equals. The matador wears his 'suit of lights'; everyone is dressed in colourful and traditional attire. And the spectre of danger hangs over the arena as in no other sport. One in three of the best matadors will die at the horns of the bull; few, if any, will escape injury altogether. Luis Freg, a famous Mexican matador who died in 1934, was gored 57 times during this career! The matador's art is to perform the traditional range of 'passes' of the bull with the cape, whilst getting as close as possible to the horns. To the majority of spectators, the *cognoscenti*, the ritual is well known. The crowd will not tolerate the matador who cuts it short, or whose performance lacks the proper and expected grace and bravery. Their disdain is demonstrated by insults and by the throwing of cushions. It may not match the anger of a South American soccer crowd, but it is mortifying for a matador. Varelito, a matador considered by Hemingway to be 'probably the best killer of his generation', returned to the ring in 1922 after a wounding without much of his old flair. In a vain attempt to please a hostile crowd he turned his back on the bull who gored him badly in the rectum.

In the perfect bullfight, though, Hemingway argued: 'no men are wounded nor killed and six bulls are put to death in a formal and ordered manner by men who expose themselves to the maximum of danger over which their ability and knowledge will allow them to triumph without casualties. In a perfect bullfight, it may be admitted frankly, some horses will be killed as well as the bulls ... but the death of the horses in the ring is an unavoidable accident and affords pleasure to no one connected with or viewing the fight except the bull, who derives supreme satisfaction from it.'

Hemingway admired the bullfighters' 'grace under pressure', but despite his valiant attempt to popularise the sport in modern times, it has never travelled far beyond the Iberian peninsula or its sphere of influence. It has long been established in Portugal and parts of France, usually in a form which spares the bull, though in 1991 the Spanish version, with the death of the bull, was made legal again in both countries. The French had previously employed different techniques to remove a cloth rosette attached by a string harness to the bull's horns. It has started up in the United States in the large Portuguese community in Massachusetts, in four forms, none involving the death of the bull. It remains popular in parts of Latin America; Mexico City has the world's largest *plaza de toros* which seats 46 000 people.

It is estimated that 30 000 bulls and calves were killed during the 1990 season in Spain. Horse deaths are uncounted.

Ironically, bullfighting's popularity in Spain may be on the wane; the numbers of corridas nearly halved from 695 to 377 between 1974 and 1985. Despite a resurgence of interest amongst young people surveys conducted by the Spanish Ministry of Culture have found that over 50 per cent of the Spanish population now favour a ban on bullfighting.

If bullfighting is losing popularity, the opposite is true of cock and dog fighting. The last particularly is seeing something of a revival in both Britain and the United States. In both counties it is illegal, but there have been few convictions. Dog fighting is legal in Japan and Afghanistan, where the sport is considered a family event – even small children attend.

Cock fighting is legal throughout Southeast Asia, and in parts of Central and South America, and some states in the

Fighting for Pleasure? A gruesome picture of dog fighting left uncollected in a chemist's shop. Dog fighting, banned in Britain and America, is on the increase. In Japan and Afghanistan it is still seen as a family sport

United States. Attached to the cocks' claws are glass or metal spurs and the cocks fight to the death. In America, there are even national cockfighting magazines with titles such as *Steel*, *Grit* and *Southern Warrior*. On American Independence Day in 1991, police in the small town of Renton, near Seattle, raided a barn being used for cock fights. Forty people were inside, and police collected over $175 000 (£100 000) of what they presumed to be betting money. Since they didn't actually see any cock fighting or gambling, only one man was arrested – for obstructing the police. But they did seize 21 roosters, a board with 10 fighting rules painted on it and a packet of metal spurs known locally as 'slashers'. In Washington State, it's a misdemeanour to encourage roosters to fight or to allow fighting on your property. According to Raymonde LaLonde, Congressman from Louisiana – where cockfighting is still legal: 'People who are involved in it feel very strongly about it.' He told the *Los Angeles Times*: 'This is part of their culture and they are not going to give it up without a fight.'

On behalf of animals, humans have decided that some so-called sports are cruel and should therefore be stopped; and some aspects of training animals for sport are wrong and should not be tolerated. At issue is the degree to which animals can be exploited in the name of human sport and there remains much inconsistency around the world. Humans can and do push themselves up to and beyond limits in search of sporting success. But that is their free choice. With animals we have to take the responsibility of choice for them; our duty is to take the right decisions on their behalf and thus to preserve civilised standards. In earlier times kings and commoners alike had no such scruples. Animals were inferior beings bred and 'educated' to carry out man's will, whatever that might be. So, they were worked and raced and jumped and pitted against other animals, of the same or even another species. But to keep things in perspective it is useful to remember that in the timescale of our development it was not very long ago that humans were entered into the sporting arena to fight to the death with lions or each other.

6 The appliance of science

Men have become the tools of their tools
H.D. THOREAU (1817–62)

A small factory in the far north of Sweden, close to the Arctic Circle, seems a long way from the cutting edge of high technology in sport. But the Nordic Sports factory in Skellefta makes many of the competition poles and javelins for the world's best vaulters and throwers.

Sergey Bubka has dominated the pole-vault since winning the world championship as a teenager in 1983. He has improved in height from 5.4 metres in 1981 to his great breakthrough of 6.12 metres on 15 March 1991, in San Sebastian – the first man over 20 feet, a historic barrier akin to the 4 minute mile. He has won the Olympic, World and European titles.

The little Swedish factory has been crucial to him. There, computer-aided critical path analysis helped produce a pole suited precisely to his height, strength and technique. As for tennis rackets, the manufacturers of modern poles have forsaken wood for carbon fibre brought directly from the NASA space programme in America. But the technology also requires human skills, to cut the fibre and wrap the segments around a long steel mandrill. Only one technician in the factory, apparently, had the precise touch Bubka required, and the pole-vaulter himself went to the factory to scrutinise

The javelin is an ancient event, but today's spears are high tech. Finland's Tina Lillak needs a good manufacturer to stay at the top

95

the process, which ends with the pole being baked in a purpose built oven controlled, inevitably, by computer. The rigorous testing which follows bends the pole double on a specially designed test bed to reproduce the stresses of competition. At the end Bubka took the pole to a local gymnasium for two days of his own testing to make sure everything was right.

To reap the rewards he believes he is due, and also to maintain his development, Bubka is moving from his native Russia to France. He feels he has to go because the political situation in Russia is not good, but also for his diet, so crucial to the top sportsman. He combines the agility of a gymnast with the pace of a sprinter (10.2 seconds for the 100 metres). How high can he go? He told Alan Hubbard of the *Observer* newspaper (June 1991) that 'with these new poles it is impossible to say. Maybe 6.40, 6.50 (metres). Who knows?' That's 21 feet, or nearly one and a half times higher than a double-decker London bus.

Technology has moved the sport of pole-vaulting, once a side-show, into a new league, as the heights scaled become gargantuan. It has done something similar with the javelin, that oldest of sporting contests. The journalist John Rodda said in 1991: 'javelin throwing could turn into a competition between the manufacturers rather than the throwers.'

Nordic Sports have also developed a javelin called the Sandvik Champion, which enabled the Finn, Seppo Raty, to throw it more than a metre beyond the then world record (to 91.98 metres) in the first competition of 1991. It marked another round in the contest, not just between the athletes, but between the manufacturers. The Hungarian manufacturer, Miklos Nemeth, had previously engineered a 'super javelin' which could stay in flight longer. John Rodda described it as 'taking the smoothness from the tail with what looks like an exaggerated sandpaper effect'. Steven Backley of Great Britain had held the world record that Raty surpassed; he said 'If there was only one recognised javelin, if anyone threw it further it would always be on their own merit, not on rival manufacturers' technological improvements. At present being

Pole-vaulters get the bends; with the right pole, Sergey Bubka leaps nearly one and a half times the height of a double-decker London bus

Muhammad Ali is 'the greatest' and George Foreman is on the floor in their world title fight in 1974. Now Ali is a shuffling shadow (*Allsport*)

The giant's playground: Sumo wrestling is more a religion than a game in its native Japan
(*Chris Cole/Allsport*)

Red flag for the USSR: 'No jump' for Larisa Berezhnaya
(*Gray Mortimore/Allsport*)

Sport for all: thousands cross the Verrazano Narrows Bridge in the New York Marathon
(*Lance Jeffrey/Allsport, USA*)

Hurrying after the hare
(*Dan Smith/Allsport*)

'What is sport to a cat is death to a mouse'. Once popular in Britain, hare coursing is now banned
(*Billy Stickland/Allsport*)

Freefall: Bechers Brook claims more victims during the 1989 Segram Grand National at Aintree, near Liverpool (*Brunskill/Bob Thomas Sports Photography*)

First fall: Gillian Maybury of Britain coming off Rum Tum Tugger at her first Badminton in 1990 (*Colorsport*)

The thrill of it all: a painting of Louis Renault and his riding mechanic Francois Szisz on their way to winning the ill-fated 1903 Paris to Madrid race
(*Walter Gotschke*)

Toy cars and sand castles: The Paris–Dakar Rally
(*Vandystadt/Allsport, France*)

Brazilian Mauricio Gugelmin,
driving for the Leyton House
team, crashes spectacularly in
the 1989 French Grand Prix
(*Pascal Ronde/Allsport*)

Riders in the sky – in stadium
cross (*JP Lenfant/Agence
Vandystadt/Allsport, France*)

world record holder does not ring true. Who is to say how far the new Sandvik would have gone the night I first gained the world record?'

Pole-vaulters and javelin throwers need speed in their run-ups and may therefore also be aided by track and field's new 'magic carpet'. In the late 1960s, the all-weather synthetic track replaced cinders, a great leap forward in technology for the sport. The 'new leotan alpha emboss track' developed in Japan is claimed to be of similar epoch making significance, according to Hiroyuki Oku, a director of one of the two companies responsible for its development. Certainly, the world sat up and took notice in August 1991 when on this new surface, the Toyko World Championships saw six men run the 100 metres in under 10 seconds. Oku told *The Times*: 'I think only four would have made it on the old surface.' A few days later, the 'carpet' worked its 'magic' on America's Mike Powell and helped him to break Bob Beamon's 23-year-old record for the long jump, and beat the oldest record in the book.

Sport is now thoroughly 'high tech'. Its everyday words and equipment would be a mystery to sportsmen and women from even just a generation ago. Today we have laminated plastics, carbon fibre, fibre glass, computer design and much more. Sport has as much to do with research chemists, mechanical engineers, industrial designers and the biology laboratory – and that's just for the equipment! – as it does with the great outdoors.

The appliance of science has resulted in racing cars hurtling around the world's circuits at more than 200 mph, and skiers flashing over artificial snow 50 per cent faster than a racehorse. The old Roman amphitheatre has been enhanced by retractable rooves and movable tracks and huge screens which show the action as it happens – and then replay it, so that performers and spectators (and judges) can watch together. The gladiators come out in skin-hugging lurex body stockings, designed for speed.

Science is all and everywhere in most sports, but nowhere

is it more obvious than in motor racing. 'Formula One has more in common with the aerospace industry than with the motor car industry,' Bob Tyrrell told us when we visited the Tyrrell Racing headquarters in Ockham, in Surrey, England.

It doesn't always work of course. Test driver Fred Gardner said in 1970, after driving the new Porsche 917: 'the computer said the car would work with narrow wheel rims, but the bloody computer wasn't strapped in the driving seat!' But most of the time, it does, and it has changed the face of sport.

Motor car (and motor cycle) racing descends directly from man's first interest in racing with the horse. Even the term 'horse power' was retained in the new machine age. The winning duo is a combined effort of speedy steed and skilful rider or driver. As we have seen the science of breeding has developed, but a horse is a horse is a horse – no more lovely, and not much quicker. Whatever Ben-Hur's chariot does in the cinema arena and however fast the cowboys race across the prairie, today's thoroughbred is still flat out at 40 mph. Today's Formula One racing car, however, bears little resem-

Inside the Tyrrell Racing HQ, where man and computer will build a 200mph Grand Prix car around this monocoque shell

98

blance to its distant relative from the late nineteenth century.

A Frenchman, Etienne Lenoir, in 1862 is credited with producing the first internal combustion engine, running on liquid hydrocarbon fuel. By the mid-1880s Gottlieb Daimler was developing the world's first petroleum powered engine. Two or three years later, Karl Benz established a factory in Germany and became one of the biggest producers of motor cars. The Industrial Revolution was turning the world's attention away from the relatively simple rural life towards things material and mechanical. The Machine Age was born, high tech was here. Despite their unreliability, and the poor road conditions, cars speedily became the stuff of dreams, offering unimagined speed and freedom. Sport was already a part of the new era of transport; races involving steam powered vehicles had been held in Europe and America in the 1870s and 1880s. Then, the 'new' vehicles were tried and one of the first known motor car races was held in 1895; it was a race between Paris and Bordeaux and back. It was won by a Frenchman, Emile Levassor, driving a Panhard-Levassor powered by a 1.2 litre Daimler engine developing 3.5 horse power and achieving an average speed of 15.25 mph (24.54 kph).

Today, there are teams of computer aided mechanics in the pits, changing a set of tyres in 5 seconds, and replacing a whole engine in a few hours. The cars are designed, prepared and monitored by computer; even starting the car requires activating a computer programme by Honda engineers — there isn't a key or a switch. The drivers, in their new safety clothing, are monitored by computer too and can receive radio advice and instruction from their headquarters in the pits. If Ayrton Senna has a problem in his Honda-McLaren, the on-board computers send details of the appropriate corrective action to the Honda personnel in the pit.

Companies spend millions of pounds, dollars, deutschmarks and yen on research and development on tyres for different weather, fuel mixtures for different altitudes, suspensions for different surfaces. Every aspect of chassis and car design depends on exhaustive testing in wind tunnels to ensure minimum drag against 'downforce' thereby optimising track adhesion and balance. Bob Tyrrell told us that: 'every pound of weight saved means one hundredth of a second faster per lap! We are all obsessive about weight, in every part and piece of the car.' There are 2500 different parts to each car (excluding the engine) and Tyrrell pointed out that 'the car at the beginning of the season bears little relation to the car at the end.'

Screenwatch; Alessandro Nannini makes sure that car and computer are in tune for the race

There have been huge leaps in motor racing technology, each soon overtaken by another. In the mid-1960s Colin Chapman was the first to build a car, the Lotus 25, with a 'monocoque' frame. This replaced the multi-tubular frame with two long aluminium sheets joined together with transverse steel bulkheads and cross members forming a 'box' which enabled the driver to sit lower down in the car and, crucially, reduced weight. Chapman also brought in the gas powered turbine engine in a Lotus in 1971. In 1976 the Tyrrell team introduced their revolutionary six-wheeled Project 34 car, which finished first and second in the Swedish Grand Prix that year. Chapman, again, added 'ground skirts' to his cars in the late 70s to prevent air escaping from the sides and thus enhance speed. However, the 'skirts' were deemed unsafe and banned in 1979.

In the same period Renault re-entered Grand Prix racing with perhaps the most significant development to date, the turbo charged engine. Its increased power brought faster speeds but led FISA (*Fédération Internationale du Sport Automobile*) – the governing body – to worry again about safety. The 'turbos' were phased out between 1986 and 1988.

The recent arrival of carbon fibre may soon prove to be the most lasting leap forward in motor racing. Already it is one of the major materials used in a Grand Prix car. Its host of applications include the bodywork, the driver's 'survival cell', the front and rear wings and the dashboard. The Tyrrell factory spends £750 000 a year on this material.

In motor racing, the car and its speed and power were

THURSDAY, JULY 4, 1889.

HOW TO MAKE A RACQUET.

Formula for Tennis Players by Which They May Save Expense.

BE YOUR OWN CARPENTER.

Build Your Own Tools and Derive a Double Satisfaction.

[FROM THE NEW YORK HERALD.]

Every boy will admit that the pleasure of making his kite, with the possible exception of the tail part, is quite equal to the satisfaction derived in flying it, and I think those who are interested in the game of tennis, or lawn tennis as it is commonly termed, to distinguish it from court tennis, will agree with me that if they could make their own racquets their zest for this beautiful sport would be commensurately increased.

SELECTING MATERIALS.

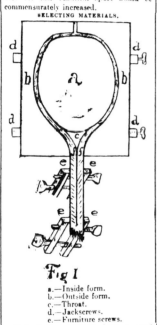

Fig I

a.—Inside form.
b.—Outside form.
c.—Throat.
d.—Jackscrews.
e.—Furniture screws.

It is indispensable to have a good racquet, else the game may not be fully enjoyed, and as that article is rather expensive, many who would otherwise be active players are simply lookers on.

Therefore I propose to add my quota to the popularity of the pastime by describing how, with a little patience and care,

DIY for tennis buffs in 1889

always vital. But high tech has altered the balance sharply away from the driver. When the legendary Juan Fangio and drivers like him pulled down their dark glass goggles over their leather flying helmets in the first championship races in the early 1950s, their own skills, strength and stamina were paramount. They had their lives in their hands. Once on the track, they were very much on their own, making their own decisions both tactical and technical. Though great skill and fitness are still required in today's drivers, theirs is more like the role of the pilot. Like the jockey in a classic race, the key factor is now the quality of the steed. James Hunt, world champion driver in 1976, said in 1979: 'What is called the World Drivers' Championship is in fact the Car Manufacturers' Championship. Drivers are becoming irrelevant these days.'

Tennis players may not be becoming irrelevant, but they too have to move with the technological times if they wish to continue to compete at the top level. Bjorn Borg must have reflected ruefully on the relevance of his skills and experience when he stepped on court again in 1991. His age, and the time he had spent in retirement were major factors against him, and the wooden racket once a perfect extension of his own arm and brain had become an anachronism.

The wooden racket endured for well over 100 years (as did the white tennis ball, another sporting dodo!) It was not sustained by governing body rules and regulations, but by the absence of obvious technical need and, until the last decade, commercial flair and muscle. In the early days a good racket was costly (rather more so than today), but the *Paris Tribune* of 1889 advised its European and American readers that: 'it is indispensable to have a good racket, else the game may not be fully enjoyed, and as that article is rather expensive, many who would otherwise be active players are simply lookers-on.' The solution was an instructive piece on: 'How to make a racket' using pine, 'a handsomely grained wood, such as curled maple or mahogany' and 'five strips of white ash'.

101

Seventy or so years later came a revolution, based on light-weight, man developed materials – first aluminium and then graphite. These could support a larger and more tightly-strung hitting area. The first into the market was the Head company with their Big Spot rackets. To ensure fair competition, regulations had to be introduced covering length of frame, width of head and area of strung surface.

The technical specifications in today's tennis magazines talk of rackets with 'elliptic interactivity', 'aerodynamic cross section', 'computer designed dual taper configuration', 'dynamic stiffness', 'torsional stability', 'vibration absorption' and – comprehensible at last – 'impact accuracy'. Clearly, a qualification in applied science is now necessary to make an informed choice!

Philippe Chatrier, who retired in 1991 as President of the ITF (International Tennis Federation), believes that technological development has changed the game for the worst, at least amongst the men: 'The brute force is taking over from the strategy, from the intelligence, from the psychology.' The nature of the sport has changed, although 'it works in favour of the women's game now'.

Because the ball was being hit harder and faster, changes were needed to help human eyes keep up. Coloured balls were one solution and we are now accustomed to day-glow yellow ones. Umpires and players also needed help with judgements of whether balls travelling at 100 mph and more were 'in' or 'out' – matters of millimetres at milliseconds. The electronic eye was introduced first at Wimbledon in 1981 and, with some refinements, has secured a place in the game's armoury. An infra-red beam between two units across the service line bleeps if the ball goes through and it is therefore 'out'. Chris Gorringe, Wimbledon's chief executive, describes it as 'an aid, a benefit, which has stood the test of time'.

Wooden skis have gone the same way as the wooden tennis rackets and vaulters' poles – into history books and museums. The first records of anyone skiing are provided by artifacts and rock drawings in Scandinavia and Serbia dated at about

102

Is it a bird, is it a plane? No, it's super-skier Jean Marc Barey with the latest downhill design

2500 BC, and the modern-day ski shape has its orgins in skis developed by the Scandinavian armies of the thirteenth century. Skis remained primarily as aids to travel until the late nineteenth century when a number of Norwegian communities began to use them in sport.

The years following the Second World War brought fast growth to the sport and the industry. Today, a bewildering array of skis are made for different conditions and levels of performance. High tech has brought laminations of a range of plastics, fibre glass, metal alloys and low friction polyethylenes bonded together in computer controlled processes. All skiing 'accessories' have enjoyed similar revolutions in design and manufacture, driven by the Gods of market share and medals. Boots no longer have birch roots to bind them to skis; they are space age and plastic, with 'front entry', 'rear entry' and 'mid entry' systems. Makers are now experimenting with all-in-one skis, boots and bindings.

Top level skiing has a supporting cast like the pit crew in Formula One racing. Teams of technicians from the manu-facturers travel the ski circuit; their task is to ensure skis are exactly right for the varying conditions of Val d'Isère, Grenoble, Serre-Chevalier and the other slopes. Hours and energy and expertise are spent honing and waxing skis ready for the race conditions. The team that gets it right may have the winner; and the winner may help sell more skis, and accessories.

The other major mountain sport is climbing, and increas-ingly, many skiers are combining both sports. But is climbing really affected by the modern, high tech world? Isn't that what mountaineers are trying to get away from?

Theirs certainly is a getaway sport. There are no crowds, few cameras, and not many sponsors make the trip! Climbing became popular – relatively speaking – in the Victorian days when it was a 'frontier' challenge and also part of 'health promoting' holidays for the upper classes. The lower classes took over the sport in the 1920s as an escape from harsh factory life.

Early this century there were technical innovations which opened up previously impossible peaks. The ten point crampon, a spiked metal attachment for boots to assist ice climbing, first appeared in 1908. During the 1920s came 'chockstones' (placed in natural cracks in the rock face with rope 'slings' threaded around them) to aid ascent where hand and foot holds were sparse; 'pitons', metal pegs hammered into the rock for the rope; and 'darabiners', oblong metal rings with a metal gate through which the rope could be slotted. Some people thought these new fangled gadgets endangered the purity of the sport. The very upper class London Alpine Club, formed in 1857, dismissed them as 'perversions' and 'monkey tricks'.

What would they say of today's array of artificial aids? The simple 'chockstone' has evolved into 'active spring loaded camming chocks', or even 'active wedging chocks'. If you have difficulty climbing the rope itself you can buy 'jummars' and 'jammers' to help. There's also a variety of 'etriers', 'expansion bolts', 'horizontal and angled pitons' and even 'pulleys'. Ropes which used to be made of natural fibres are now far stronger, lighter and more elastic, in nylon. Safety helmets are constructed from lightweight plastics borrowed from industry. The climbing boot has been transformed as severely as the old plimsoll.

The benefits have been appreciated by the practitioners. British mountaineer, Doug Scott, told us the boots were a direct spin-off from skiing: 'They make it virtually impossible to get frost bite in the toes and feet, which was a very real problem for climbers in the 1940s, 50s and 60s.' Undoubtedly, many limbs and lives have been saved by the new boots, weather proof clothing, lightweight tents and even portable cooking stoves.

In Los Angeles in 1984, the hot rumour in the Olympic Village among the archers of different nations was that the Chinese had developed a revolutionary new bow, said to be unbeatable. There was excitement and some fear as the competition

approached, but when the Chinese appeared they seemed to have perfectly ordinary bows. A little advanced on Robin Hood's, but nothing special. Whether or not they were different we may never know, but the Chinese won no medals.

No such gossip was evident in the Games' cycling fraternity. But, come the day, out rode the US team with new, strange looking machines with large front wheels, and cleaned up medals all over the place. Later, of course, we learned that they had another innovation, one not then outside the laws – blood doping – and maybe, that helped them more than their high tech bikes.

Sport today is consumed by high technology. The two need each other to develop. But, an edge in equipment can be more important than skill, fitness or experience. Sport must be careful to ensure that the real competition remains on the track, in the field or in the arena and not in the manufacturers' labs and workshops.

Super bikes! The Italian team racing in the 1986 World Championships

7 The highest stakes of all

Human beings inspire more fear in me than Arctic expeditions
SIR RANULPH FIENNES, EXPLORER AND WRITER, JULY 1991

For some sports, you have to take your life in your hands, and sometimes other people's too! To participate can mean to dice with danger and death; undoubtedly there is a ghastly pleasure for the spectator in imagining what might happen. The downhill racer at Aspen, Colorado, has two minutes on the edge of the mountain, alone with his skis and skill. The Formula One driver is a circuit racer, at speeds of over 200 mph, in a specially constructed car – made, probably, in Britain. The climber, or mountaineer, does very little at speed – except, perhaps fatally, to fall – but appears to cling to life and rock by the fingertips. The boxer goes into the ring to hurt, and get hurt – even if, technically, the aim is to score points.

Why do they do it? The well-known response by the mountain climber is 'because it's there'. The racers on snow or concrete savour the speed and excitement. The American skier, Andy Mill, now looks at sport from comfortable retirement (with his wife, the tennis star Chris Evert, also retired) and he says such people 'are born with a certain sense of excitement. Some people like things that are a little more conservative, other people like to push the limit a little bit – I have always been one of those people who would like to walk that final line.'

Smoke, fire and death at the Le Mans 24-hour race in 1955, after a Mercedes ploughed into the crowd. Mercedes withdrew from motor racing until 1988

If the risks are high, so are the thrills, and therein lies the key motivation. All you need is a curious kind of courage. As G.K. Chesterton remarked: 'Courage is almost a contradiction in terms. It means a strong desire to live taking the form of a readiness to die.'

Standing underneath the huge ski jump at Holmenkollen outside Oslo, or watching the men's downhill at Aspen, Colorado, it sometimes seems amazing that death is not a regular visitor. But injuries at least are an everyday hazard. Andy Mill again: 'I got hurt a lot, too much. I had nine knee operations, two broken legs, a broken arm, a broken neck and a broken back.'

'You don't think about fear, or how dangerous it's going to be because you know you have trained for it,' the Austrian downhill skier Peter Wirnsberger told us. 'I know what I am able to do and I know I can do it. That is the most important point.' Wirnsberger believes that, for a sport with such speeds and risks, the training and preparation are vital: 'You need a perfect body, you have to be in good shape.' But there is also an essential instinct, or what Wirnsberger called a 'feeling', that the best downhill racers have: 'They don't have to think, if there is something going on on the slope, they just react. That's in a time difference of hundredths of a second, and you can't explain how you thought about it, and how you made your decision, how to handle it, it is just you feel it and you do the right thing.' Wirnsberger stresses too, the need for mental planning of a race beforehand 'to get your mind focused'.

In the blue riband event, the downhill, top competitors reach speeds of 80 mph. Yet Steve Podborski of Canada, the joint world champion in 1982, says: 'Downhill skiing is the classic fight or fright syndrome. The only thing I want to do when I am going fast is – go faster.' Echoing Wirnsberger, he told us: 'You don't think. There is no thought process in skiing. You react like an animal.'

The great British Grand Prix driver of the 1950s, Stirling Moss, used to talk of a driver's 'sixth sense'. Drivers and racers operate at what to most of us are dangerous speeds, when not everything can be predicted. In these speed sports the unexpected happens very, very quickly. What protects the racer or driver is that amalgam of skill and experience which marks the top performer. Perhaps therefore it shouldn't be surprising that the biggest danger is often to the spectators.

In the early days motor races were held on roads, but there were a number of accidents, especially to spectators, because drivers lacked the technique to keep control of the cars at speed on the often unsuitable road surfaces. The 1903 Paris to Madrid race was stopped at Bordeaux and abandoned because of the high incidence of accidents. Soon after that, racing on roads was banned altogether and the racing teams and the sport moved to the enclosed circuits we know today.

Fifty years later, the sport had another safety crisis linked to technique and technology. The 1950s witnessed an unprecedented series of tragedies as high tech engine and chassis development outstripped drivers' abilities and control. In 1952, 13 people died in Weyburg, Germany, when a car left the track. The following year 15 were killed at the Argentine Grand Prix. In 1955, 83 died and over 100 were injured when a Mercedes flew over the safety barrier into the crowd at the Le Mans 24-hour race. Mercedes then withdrew from motor racing and did not return until 1988. In 1957, 13 died (six of them children) when a Ferrari went out of control in Italy's famous Mille Miglia endurance race; this marked the end of those races, after 30 years.

There have been many other tragedies, large and small, over the years. Twenty-one Grand Prix drivers have lost their lives in the last 40 years. Participants and spectators alike have wanted speed and danger, and car racing has given all this and more. Speeds close to 100 mph were being reached by the late 1920s. But protective clothing for drivers remained non-existent; the early cloth caps had been replaced only by leather racing caps, goggles and overalls, which gave little protection against injury. Similarly, a few straw bales and wooden fences were all that stood between spectators and the nearly 2000 lbs of metal hurtling round the track at close to 100 mph.

These days, however, Grand Prix motor car racing is considered by its exponents to be a safe sport. Since the tragedies of the 1950s, there has been an emphasis on safety and precaution from the sport's governing bodies. Cars and circuits are safer, there has not been a driver death in Formula One racing since 1986 and few serious injuries. Today's drivers feel they are in much less danger in races or in practice sessions than their counterparts in previous years. For Bob Tyrrell of Tyrrell Racing, there have been 'three main factors in making the sport safe – advanced composite technology; safety features around the tracks; and the high computer technology, making for safe and very accurate calculations for each race and track.'

Tyrrells' number one driver, Stefano Modena, gave us this view: 'I am in greater danger each time I drive my own car than in a Formula One race. On the track, I have no cars coming towards me, and I am with experienced, professional drivers. And we all know our cars and their limits.' Graham Wilkie, who once held the world speed record for downhill skiing, makes a similar point: 'Many think of us as eccentrics,

A risky career!

110

freaks, kamikaze people, (but) driving a London cab is more dangerous.'

Of course, risks remain. When all the plans have been made, all the parts of the car checked, adjustments made for the track and the weather conditions, the computer race programme evaluated, and the team talk has thrashed out all the possible last details, every driver knows there is still one final factor that cannot be evaluated – Murphy's Law (Sod's Law to some) – which is respected and feared by any participant in a dangerous sport. Few followers of Formula One will forget the last race of the 1986 series, in Adelaide, for example. Nigel Mansell in his Williams had only to finish 4th or better to clinch the Drivers' World Championship title. Man and machine appeared to be in perfect harmony, as they had been in most races that season. But the car blew a tyre on the 64th lap. Mansell's dreams and the team's were shattered in a split second; all Mansell himself could do, having brilliantly brought his car to a stop, was to shrug his shoulders.

The long apprenticeships required to progress in motor racing enable participants, to a significant degree, to accustom themselves to the risks of serious injury and death and to learn how to minimise those risks. But it would be foolish to deny the danger for top drivers in every contest and practice. The Argentinian, Juan Fangio, is thought by some to have been the greatest of all, but note these comments he made about his serious accident at Monza in 1952: 'I passed six cars on the opening lap and was going well on the second. Heading into the second corner … I got my line wrong and I touched the low barrier on the inside, the car began to slide and instead of correcting it early I let the slide develop, my instant reaction being that I would correct it later on the left side of the road. But due to fatigue this reaction was wrong.

'I hit the very last of the line of straw bales … they had been there for years and alternate rain and sun had baked them like stone. When the Maserati struck I was astonished – it instantly flipped. I remember gripping the wheel tight and then my grip being broken and flying through the air towards

111

the trees. I remember smelling grass, and then I lost consciousness.'

Fangio will be remembered for winning five world titles in the 1950s, a feat never since bettered. Stirling Moss describes him as 'sheer genius'. But even he could make such a mistake, with such devastating consequences.

The Grand Prix driver John Watson described his sport, in July 1981, as 'an artistic form of bear baiting, in which the beast has to be teased and coaxed and teased some more, but never so much that it can bite back, because it bites back bad'. Martin Donnolly knows this, but he cannot stay away. He is a young Formula One driver who suffered multiple injuries in a crash at 170 mph in his Lotus at the Jerez circuit in Spain in 1990. The immediate medical judgement was that he could not survive. He did. He says now that he wants to return to the Grand Prix track as soon as he can: 'It's the only thing I know how to do. The thought of getting back into motor racing is the only thing that keeps me going. It beats working for a living.'

Motorcycle racing has a similar history and is probably more dangerous. The risks are higher for the rider with no cockpit or roll bar and without the stability of four wheels. The sport has grown with the technology, the sponsorship, the media – and the personalities. Speed and danger still go hand in hand and it seems the more dangerous the circuit the more attractive the race, both for spectators and for riders.

The Isle of Man 'Tourist Trophy', better known simply as the TT, illustrates the point. This small island off the west coast of England was first used as a practice venue for cars and bikes in the late nineteenth century for the early wave of road races. Then, British legislation restricted such races on the mainland and limited speeds. The Isle of Man was unaffected and responded to the manufacturers' desire for road space. The British companies in particular needed a venue in order to keep up with their Continental competition. The move to enclosed circuits for cars limited the world 'market' for the island, but they were able to establish an

Two wheels are even more dangerous than four

official motorcycle race in 1907 and the tradition remains today. Over the years the TT races have been costly in lives – a total of 166 riders have been killed since 1907. There has been regular pressure to ban the race, most recently for example in 1985 when five riders were killed; last year (1991), there were another six deaths. Nevertheless, the race lives on, something of an anachronism in a sport now based largely on enclosed circuits and with proper care for its safety record.

The top drivers and riders are also top competitors – like the best in every sport. They badly want to perform well and win. Ayrton Senna maintains it is 'all down to the fine tuning; the fine tuning of my car, its chassis and balance, and my body, my heart and my brain. To be at my peak I need to have them all together at their peaks at the same time. For me it is a task and a challenge every time I drive.'

For such men, danger and injury and even death are part of the fabric of life. Fangio said this about the death of a team mate during the 1954 German Grand Prix: 'It was very difficult to drive afterwards, but that was our profession.' Danger also draws the crowds. In America the Indianapolis 500 is the greatest motor race of the year, notable for its spills

113

and thrills. In 1976, A.J. Foyt, one of its regulars, said, 'on the day of a big motor race, a lot of people want you to sign something just before you get into the car, just so they can say they got your last autograph.'

That voyeuristic excitement, the thought of blood, is certainly in the minds of the crowd watching a bullfight – and it is not just the blood of the bull. Of the 125 or so top matadors since 1700, no fewer than 40 have died in the ring. But machismo is part of the bullfighters' creed. 'The coward is not a man,' according to Pedro Romero, the first of the great modern bullfighters, 'and to fight bulls men are necessary.' In 1946 Manolete, another famous bullfighter, said: 'I know very well what they want, and one of these days I might just give it to them to keep the bastards happy.' The novelist Joseph Conrad wrote that 'the aficionados go for one reason: to see the almost death of the matadors.'

Some regard boxing too as a sporting anachronism, another

The suit of lights becomes a shroud. One in three top matadors die on the horns of the bull

114

dangerous one. In the early prize fighting days fights were over when one man was unable to continue fighting, when he could no longer get 'up to the mark'. The phrase lingers on today, in common parlance. For every fight the 'mark' was made at the beginning, in the centre of the area forming the 'ring'.

But boxing has always been big sport and big business. It was long one of the 'hungry' sports, a way out of poverty. The temptation was to fight too often and to go on too long. In the 1920s and 30s fighters might take on three and four opponents a day! As recently as the late 1940s, the British heavyweight, Bruce Woodcock, carried on for seven fights blind in one eye. He lost sight in the other after a torrid defeat at the hands of the American Joe Baksi, who also broke his jaw. Woodcock and his manager and advisers kept quiet about the eye. They all needed the extra pay days.

Governing bodies have to protect fighters against themselves, their friends and their public, and in recent years stringent and regular medical checks have been introduced. The experienced boxing writer, Colin Hart, thinks that in Britain, at least, the sport 'is now as safe as they can make it, without diluting it further.' The punishing 15 round bouts had their day after a Korean boxer, Deuk-Koo-Kim, died in the 14th round of a world lightweight title fight in 1982. The WBC (World Boxing Council) was the first to change to 12 round contests, and others have followed suit. However, many believe that saftey wasn't the only reason; that the change was also motivated by the demands of TV as shorter fights fitted better into TV schedules.

But 12 round fights are not the panacea, as Hart acknowledges. In September 1980, Johnny Owen of Wales fought Lupe Pintor of Mexico for the world bantamweight title. It was held in the Los Angeles Olympic stadium in the Mexican quarter of the city. 'Everyone was searched on the way in, ' Hart recalls, 'and they had a rare haul of knives and guns.' Owen was a skinny, brave and clever boxer, but he was knocked out by Pintor in the 12th round of a tough contest

in front of a highly partisan crowd – 'like an audience out of a B-movie,' Hart recalls. He followed Owen on his stretcher out of the arena; 'I noticed with horror the blood seeping out of Owen's ear.' With equal horror, he saw the urine thrown out of plastic cups on to the stricken boxer. Owen never recovered consciousness and died, back home in his native Welsh valley of Merthyr, some six weeks later.

Los Angeles, 19 September 1980; the Welsh boxer Johnny Owen is down and out in the 12th round of his world title fight against Mexico's Lupe Pintor

116

Do boxers ever fear the outcome of a fight? In the most macho of sporting worlds, such emotions have to be concealed. The British boxer Nigel Benn says: 'I keep going all the time; bang, crash, bang, crash. I don't fear nothing if I'm in good shape, even when they shout "Benn, it's your time". But if I think I haven't prepared myself right, then I'm in the wrong frame of mind. Otherwise the ring don't hold no fear for me. Why be in the game if you're scared?'

The change to 12 rounds would not have saved Johnny Owen, but today's careful medical examinations would have uncovered the fact that he had a thin skull. They would also have prevented Bruce Woodcock risking the loss of his other eye. Boxing's safety record was raised dramatically again, at the time of writing, when Michael Watson required emergency brain surgery after his defeat by Chris Eubank in the WBO (World Boxing Organisation) super middleweight world title fight in September 1991 in London.

Further safety moves are often suggested for boxing, and they include banning it altogether. Growing sentiment to ban boxing comes from neurological research indicating that regular boxing can cause serious damage to the brain. Muhammad Ali, the great heavyweight champion who helped bring boxing to its current popularity, has become a shuffling symbol of the sport's possible costs, suffering from Parkinson's Syndrome which can be caused by Parkinson's disease but can also result from injuries caused by fighting. Dr Stanley Fahn said in *Muhammad Ali: His Life and Times* by Thomas Hauser: 'Muhammad Ali doesn't have Parkinson's disease as has sometimes been reported ... his physical condition resulted from repeated blows to his head over time.' According to the *Journal of the American Medical Association*, 10 to 15 per cent of professional boxers have chronic brain damage, marked by dementia, memory loss, slurred speech, tremor and abnormal gait. To reduce risk some suggest shorter rounds, a larger interval between rounds, and different weight gloves (interestingly, opposing sides claim greater safety for both lighter and heavier gloves). One safety innovation, headguards, has already been introduced in amateur boxing (and therefore in the Olympics). With any or all of these, boxing could be safer. But, Colin Hart says: 'people go because there is an element of danger. They go to see knock-outs, to see men hurt. That's why the heavyweights are the most popular.'

In the USA there is no federal commission watching over the sport like the British Board of Control. Different States have their own regulatory bodies with different rules; some, like Wyoming, have nothing and often even common safeguards do not apply. Aaron Pryor, a fine boxer in recent years, fought there recently because it was the only place he could fight. Like Woodcock 40 years ago, he was blind in one eye!

The American tv commentator, Howard Cosell, said in 1982: 'Professional boxing is no longer worthy of civilised society. It's run by self-serving crooks, who are called promotors. You'll never clean it up ... mud can never be clean.'

'Boxing is not morally defensible,' says Colin Hart, but he does not favour trying to ban it. 'If it were banned, it would just go underground. The demand is so strong. It is dangerous – that's what people come to see. Surely, it's better to have it out in the open and then exercise the right and proper controls?'

Climbing is the sport most 'out in the open'. Indeed it is far too exposed for any but the hardiest enthusiasts, but there are many, many of them around the world. The waiting list for a climbing trip to the main Himalayan peaks is at least two years – so it is not done on impulse. And you do not usually go alone. Such 'trips' are carefully planned expeditions, and often multi-national. Anyone can climb on their own, of course, and on impulse, if using their rather more friendly, local escarpments. But the dangers in the sport are obvious and real. We talked to Doug Scott, the famous British mountaineer who specialises in alpine style climbing. He is a veteran of 25 Himalayan peaks, including four Everest expeditions. In 1979 Scott was the first climber to reach the top of Kanchenjunga (8584 metres) without Sherpa support and without oxygen.

Why does he do it? 'To say "because it is there", is a bit fatuous,' Scott explained, 'but through risking your life you become alive. By going to the limits of endurance you come back a changed, altered person, more awake and renewed – you are able to deal better and more objectively with the ups and downs of ordinary life.'

The risks in mountaineering are higher than in Grand Prix racing or boxing for that matter. More than half of Doug Scott's climbing partners have died; 'Not all on expeditions, but most on mountain ranges.' Scott himself is fatalistic; 'Sometimes it's almost as if it is written that a climber would die on a particular expedition.' Scott has even known climbers who have dreamed of their own death beforehand. But still 'It does not make me want to give up mountaineering or climbing.'

American football is said to be the most dangerous team sport of all. According to Steve Courson, former player with the Pittsburgh Steelers, the injury rate is 100 per cent. He says: 'The average lifespan or mortality rate of a professional football player who has played four or more years in the NFL has ranged between 54 and 58, which, in my opinion, speaks for the accumulative effect of the damage and the lifestyle that the game and the pressure of the game puts on the players.' In all contact sports injury is part of the game and many retire early, with limbs, if not life, impaired.

For many of us in our TV armchairs, danger is what turns the controls. Some cannot bear to watch, but most of us can and do. It is hard to say which risk is the most frightening: inching up a mountain or skiing down it at 80 mph; driving at twice that speed; or going just half a 3 minute round with Mike Tyson. But the inherent danger makes them all compulsive viewing.

Colin Hart notes that 'if you get a collision in soccer or rugby, on comes the trainer with his magic sponge. A quick dash of water, maybe a spray of something, and the player carries on. Boxing is far more careful than that. In particular, after a knock-out no one is allowed even to spar for 28 days.

And all boxers have a full medical, including a brain scan, at least once a year.'

The comparison is fair, up to a point. Every sport needs proper controls to protect the well-being of its participants, if only from themselves, or from their coaches. Yelena Mukhina, the Russian gymnast who broke her neck training for the 1980 Olympics and remains in a wheelchair, says: 'My problem was, I could not say no to my coach.' A Soviet official has written that 'there is not a single world class gymnast performing today who has not been seriously injured.' The chief responsibility lies with managers and coaches. The enthusiasm of youth needs to be controlled and channelled. Coaching programmes and techniques must be based on a thorough knowledge of their subject's physical ability, particularly in sports where talent flowers early and bodies are still growing. Andrea Jaeger and Tracey Austin are well-known tennis casualties in recent years in this respect.

The sports discussed in this chapter have a heady mixture of danger and death. They have and need a government health warning. But sport at the top is especially full of risk. Many doctors share the view expressed to us by the Russian surgeon Yuly Krelin that: 'Professional sport has nothing to do with health.' A high responsibility rests with coaches and administrators to help make sport safe for all.

American football, the most dangerous team sport of all; USC v Notre Dame, 1985, at the Los Angeles Coliseum

121

8 Pride and prejudice

Men trifle with their business and their politics; but never trifle with their games . . . it brings truth home to them . . .

GEORGE BERNARD SHAW

The TV cameras whirred outside the Houses of Parliament in London SW1. Peter Hain, the young and newly elected MP for Neath, in South Wales, but brought up in Pretoria, South Africa, smiled for the camera; 'It's great news!' he said, 'I'm delighted that South Africa is back in the Olympic Movement.' Hain had been one of the key activists in the anti-apartheid campaign since the late 60s. That evening, in July 1991, the sudden readmission of South Africa to world sport was a major news story all round the world. Two days later, they were readmitted to international cricket; the same week President Bush removed most of the trade sanctions against South Africa. It was 31 years since their athletes last competed in the Olympic Games, in Rome in 1960. For three decades, sport had been in the vanguard of the political debate whenever South Africa was discussed; now the conflict between the sporting and the political ideals had apparently come to an end. It is not the only time such ideals have been in conflict.

In 1980 the Olympic Games were staged in Moscow. The Soviet Union had invaded Afghanistan and President Carter decided that Americans should show their displeasure by not going to Moscow; the United States officially boycotted the

Who guards the guardian's rights? Golf under the gun at Rhodesia's Leopard Rock Hotel. Normal play wasn't resumed until the end of the civil war in 1980

123

Games. Sport was politics – the gesturing kind.

Prime Minister Margaret Thatcher took a less aggressive route by *asking* British competitors not to go. The British hockey, rowing and equestrian teams withdrew, but most sports attended, following the lead of the BOA. The British team in Moscow included Colin Moynihan, later to be Minister for Sport under Mrs Thatcher, and Sebastian Coe, later to be vice-chairman of the same government's Sports Council. Seb was quoted at the time with saying, '1980 will be the year when the world's politicians will be able to sit down and say they successfully dismantled sport.'

In 1969, El Salvador and Honduras played each other at soccer in qualifying matches for the 1970 World Cup. The first game was played in Honduras. The night before the game a crowd of Hondurans gathered outside the hotel where the Salvadoran team was staying and set off fire crackers, leaned on car horns, and beat on sheets of tin all night. The sleepless Salvadorans lost 1–0. The first casualty occurred when 18-year-old Amelia Bolanios, after seeing El Salvador lose on TV, shot herself in the heart. The next day the Salvadoran newspaper *El Nacional* said: 'The young girl could not bear to see her fatherland brought to its knees.' Amelia's funeral procession was televised and the President of the republic and his ministers walked behind the coffin. Some weeks later the Honduras team went to San Salvador for the return match. They were given the same type of pre-game treatment as their rivals, including having rotten eggs and dead rats thrown into their rooms. El Salvador won the next day's match 3–0. As the Honduras team was taken back to the airport in armoured cars through crowds holding up pictures of their national heroine, Amelia Bolanios, the Honduras coach, Mario Griffin, said: 'We're awfully lucky that we lost.' The next morning a plane dropped a bomb over Tegucigalpa, Honduras. Then came word that the Salvadoran army was attacking over the border between the two countries. The soccer war lasted 100 hours, 6000 people were killed, more than 12000 wounded, and thousands lost their homes.

In 1968, at the Olympic Games in Mexico City, sport's greatest single event staged an exciting 200 metres final. Tommie Smith and John Carlos, two brilliant black Americans, came first and second. This was sport, at the highest level – literally – for these were the Games at such altitude that artificial times and distances were set that remained in the record books for some years to come. The crowd, hoarse from the final, were hushed for the medal ceremony – that

'Black Power' enters the arena. Tommie Smith (centre) and John Carlos make their clenched fist salute as their national anthem is played at the Mexico Olympics in 1968. Lord Burleigh (in front of the rostrum) keeps his eyes front

unique formality, savoured only by home crowds, medal winners and their families and coaches and those dignitaries whose turn it is in the spotlight, handing over the medals and flowers. Suddenly, out of a clear blue sky, sport became politics. For Smith and Carlos raised their black gloved fists to the heavens above, in what had just become known as the salute of the Black Power movement in America.

The two claimed afterwards that their demonstration was not planned. They just saw the moment and grabbed it. An Olympic victory rostrum was too good a political opportunity to miss. Their signal, their salute, their statement flashed around the world, grabbing the TV screens of millions of the world's citizens. Carlos said later: 'We are sort of show horses out there for the white people. They give us peanuts, pat us on the back and say: "Boy, you did us fine".'

In 1967, in New Zealand, the great Springboks (the South African rugby team) toured. This was a clash between the two giants of the rugby union world (and rich irony in the traditional name of the New Zealanders – the All Blacks). There were demonstrations at every match against the South African policy of apartheid. Banners went up all round the rugby world – 'Keep politics out of sport'.

Throughout the twentieth century, these and other examples have shown that sport and politics have always touched, sometimes spitting and sometimes embracing. At international level, sporting contests are about national pride, which must have something to do with politics. It applies even to cricket, that most mannered of games. In 1932, the England tour of Australia became known as the 'bodyline tour'. The fierce bowling of England's Harold Larwood in particular, believed to be directed at the batsman's body rather than his wicket, caused a rumpus. Both governments considered intervention and the Australians even contemplated leaving the Commonwealth.

Can sport ever be distanced from politics? The authors of this book have a bias which should not be concealed; we believe that sport is part of life and reflects, inevitably, its best and sometimes its worst aspects. Sport inspires and despairs us all. Like any part of life, it must play a part in the political process. Nowhere is it illustrated better than at the 1936 Olympics. After what is arguably one of the great public relations coups of all time, Hitler said: 'Sport and chivalrous competition awakens the best human qualities ... It helps to strengthen the bonds of peace between the nations. May the Olympic flame therefore never be extinguished.' But before his election, he had dismissed the Olympic Movement as 'an invention of Jews and freemasons'.

The story began in 1932. After a postal ballot, the IOC had selected Berlin (over Barcelona) as the host city for the 1936 Games. Berlin had been scheduled to host the 1916 Games, but there had been war instead. The German Organising Committee had its first meeting in Berlin's town hall on 24 January 1933. Six days later Hitler came to power and the Committee and the IOC had rather more on their hands than they had bargained for.

Over the next three years, controversy and the Games marched in step. Should the 'Nazi Olympics' take place? Should the British, still regarded as the home of sport and of fair play and sportsmanship, send a team? Other nations, and especially the Americans, debated the issue.

In Britain and the USA the public stance was that governments should not interfere, or comment. But the British Ambassador in Berlin, Sir Eric Phipps, warned consistently that Hitler was planning the Games as a political device. They were going to be a huge spectacle, lavish and efficient, to show the world that the new Germany was an organisational and cultural force to be reckoned with. They were, and they did.

But before the torch was lit – a touch of theatre devised specially for the Berlin Olympics by Carl Diem, Secretary General of the Organising Committee, in 1934 and retained ever since – there were moral issues to be aired abroad. Sports loving men and women were asked to judge whether the Olympic Games were worth the candle.

127

The central issue was the Nazi government's persecution of the Jewish race. To understand events we have to capture the context. History has made a conclusive judgement about the Third Reich on later evidence, after the events of 1933–36. At the time, matters were not quite so clear cut. The mood was against another war; countries wanted peace and good relations with their neighbours, including Hitler's Germany. Many saw what they were allowed to see or perhaps what they wanted to see.

They saw, for example, a Germany restoring itself, its pride and its confidence, and its economy. They saw a country at once loud and passionate in its new creed and also careful of its international image.

Professor Allen Guttman in *The Games Must Go On* says: 'The discrepancy between Nazi doctrine and Olympic rule-book was a central issue' when the IOC assembled in Vienna on 7 June 1933. Count Baillet-Latour of France had been re-elected President at the meeting; he and the American members questioned the German representatives about Jewish participation in the 1936 Games. After consultation with Berlin, a written guarantee was secured that: 'All the laws regulating the Olympic Games shall be observed. As a principle German Jews shall not be excluded from German teams at the Games ...' It was also agreed that Jewish members of other nations' teams would not be disallowed.

One of the American IOC members, General Charles Sherrill, later recorded, in a letter: 'It was a trying fight ... The Germans yielded slowly, very slowly. First they conceded that other nations could bring Jews. Then, after that fight was over, telephone calls came from Berlin (saying) that no publication should be given to their government's backdown on Jews, but only the vague statement that they agreed to follow our rules ... Then I went at them hard, insisting that as they had expressly excluded Jews, now they must expressly declare the Jews not even be excluded from German teams ... Finally they yielded because they found I had lined up the necessary votes.' As anywhere in politics, votes are everything;

Two of the most powerful symbols of the century – the Olympic flame and the Nazi swastika – are juxtaposed. Hitler dares and wins in Berlin, 1936

129

and this was the guarantee that was to survive if somewhat shakily through to the Games. It was a doctrine that depended upon the Nazis keeping their word. It would have meant affording their Olympians, including Jews, a freedom absent from the new Nazi system. Such an outcome was never possible. But sports people wanted to believe that it could be, and that the Olympics would have special treatment.

However, in Nazi Germany, as later in South Africa, the evidence was there to be found; sport was becoming increasingly politicised, in common with all other parts of German society. The 1936 Olympic Games were planned and run not by the IOC, not by the German Organising Committee, but by Hitler and his henchmen.

The US Olympic Committee (USOC) decided attend the Berlin Games, but, fuelled by newspaper reports of events in Germany, the public campaign against the decision grew. The US government would not get involved, even though they were receiving the same sort of advice from their diplomats in Berlin as the British were. The spotlight fell – not for the last time – on the USOC chairman, Avery Brundage, a strong advocate of the Berlin Olympic cause.

According to Duff Hart-Davis, in *Hitler's Olympics*, the US Consul General George S. Messersmith, cabled in 1935: 'It is inconceivable that the United States Olympic Committee should continue its stand that sport in Germany is non-political.' As debate raged on, Brundage was moved to release a pamphlet entitled 'Fair play for American Athletes', which stressed that the athlete should not be made 'a martyr to a cause not his own' and should not become embroiled in 'the present Jew-Nazi altercation'. As Professor Guttman notes: 'the entire problem, in his (Brundage's) eyes, was that opponents of the Nazi regime really wanted a boycott to undermine Nazism; they meant to use the Games as a political weapon.' In part, Brundage was right. American Jews in particular were ready to express their opposition to Hitler in any way possible. But Brundage had made the mistake of believing that *all* those who disagreed with him did so for their

130

own political motives. He ignored a Gallup poll in March 1935 which showed 43 per cent of the population in favour of a boycott. He also ignored the real political motivation behind the preparations in Berlin.

Brundage's attitudes and reactions had their echoes years later when some of his successors in sports administration came to defend sporting contacts with South Africa. He had begun a tradition that placed sporting principle before political reality. Throughout his life Brundage never forgot this bitter struggle. He most remembered 'the viciousness of the contest to prevent a US team from participating'. In Britain there were similar protests between 1933 and 1936, but the BOA stayed firm and steadfast in the IOC and Berlin camp. Hart-Davis notes that 'a glance at the hierarchy of the BOA shows how aristocratic the direction of athletics was in Britain at that date.' On 17 March the whole Council signed a letter to *The Times* saying that 'The British Olympic Council are convinced that in sending a team to Berlin they are acting in the best interests of sport.' They also referred to: 'this very critical stage in world affairs' – surely, a political judgement!

When the British team paraded at the opening ceremony, none of the athletes raised their arm in the Fascist salute to Hitler as they marched past. Immediately before them, the French team had made the salute, to thunderous applause from the crowd. *The Times*, noting the difference, said the British, simply turning 'eyes right' had looked 'stately and British'. Throughout the Games there was uncertainty amongst some visitors whether or not to join the general German rush to make the Fascist salute on every possible occasion. Even the IOC members were divided.

Looking back, the IOC emerges with little credit from the Berlin experience. They had a difficult hand, but they played it weakly. Perhaps the modern Olympic movement was still too young to flex it muscles properly; perhaps, Hitler had a sharper perception of Olympic power than the IOC. There appears to have been no real attempt to bargain with him. (The negotiations over the Vienna 'guarantee' were carried

131

out over the telephone, and apparently with officials.) The Germans would have lost face (and a great opportunity) if the IOC had moved the Games elsewhere, but this was a trump card apparently not even flourished. Hitler planned and organised the Olympic Games for his own political ends and perhaps only the flashing shape of Jesse Owens saved the face of Olympism from complete disgrace.

Organisationally, the Berlin Games were all that was promised. Everything ran to time and all the facilities and the city itself were dressed specially. Very specially. The usual anti-Jewish hoardings had all been removed. In the shops foreign newspapers and magazines which had all been banned since the Nazis came to power were openly on sale. The citizens had all been enjoined to make visitors feel welcome. Maybe, they would all have done so anyway.

Were the 1936 Games a major propaganda coup? Opinions vary. Pierre de Coubertin remarked that they were organised 'with Hitlerian strength and discipline', and that was a common impression. But it is a black man, Jesse Owens, a hero among heroes and heroines, who remains the icon of the Games for most people. No Aryan could catch him and had the Games been cancelled, or if the USA had not attended, we would have been denied the memory and achievements of one of the greatest heroes sport has known. When Jesse Owens mounted the rostrum to collect his gold medal for the 100 metres, Hitler could scarcely control his anger. In the box with Hitler was Baldur Von Schirach, only 28, the Reich Youth leader. He recorded later that the German Chancellor observed that 'the Americans should be ashamed of themselves, letting negroes win their medals for them. I shall not shake hands with this negro.'

But racism and prejudice was not only rampant in Germany; indeed had it not been endemic in Britain and America and many other countries at the same time, perhaps the worst of Hitler's terrible crimes could have been prevented. Jesse Owens was to remark later: 'I came back to my native country and I could not ride in the front of the bus ... I was not invited to shake hands with Hitler, but I was not invited to the White House to shake hands with the President either.' And Professor Guttman notes that: 'neither Owens nor any other black champion was pictured in the *Atlanta Constitution*, the most liberal of southern newspapers.'

Thirty-two years later, Smith and Carlos' clenched fist salute in Mexico City was a gesture of frustration at the racism still alive in the United States. Cassius Clay came back from the Rome Olympics with a gold medal but discovered it was not a badge of acceptability in society. Richard Durham records Clay as saying: 'My memory of the summer of 1960 is not the hero's welcome, the celebrations ... the Mayor, the Governor ... but that night I stood on the Jefferson County Bridge and threw my Olympic gold medal down to the bottom of the Ohio River.' And with a delicacy which matches his stride, the Tanzanian former world record miler, Filbert Bayi, once said: 'Humanity is more important than winning a gold medal. What I pray for is not a gold medal but equality.'

Since the beginning of this century, black people have seen and used sport as a way out of poverty and racial prejudice. The first black baseball player to break into the major leagues in America was Jackie Robinson, as late as 1946. He had to endure years of abuse, and open hatred, with the Brooklyn Dodgers, including some from his own side. Black players are now commonplace in baseball and American football, but in football whispers persist that positions like quarterback are for intelligent white men rather than blacks. Art Shell, head coach to the Los Angeles Raider, is only the second ever black American football coach (after Fritz Pollard, briefly, in 1922 with the Hammond Pros). Shell says: 'I hope it does help other minority coaches. But it'll only mean something if I'm successful.' In Britain, at a time when a Brazilian black called Pele was the most famous footballer in the world, it was still being said that blacks were unable to play football because they had not got the thighs, or the 'bottle', or even that they did not like the rain!

133

Sport has played a part in both building and knocking down prejudice, and nowhere more so in recent times than in South Africa. By the 1960s, some (but not all) international sporting bodies were not prepared to sacrifice their principles to suit one government. The principle was, that under South Africa's apartheid system, sporting development and competition was neither free nor fair nor equal. The Pretoria government had the Third Reich penchant for secrecy but could not, and indeed would not, conceal the nature of life in the republic. South Africa found itself on the outside of many sports and competitions, exiled by international sports bodies like FIFA and the IOC. Later, governments picked up the baton; by now they too had learned the lesson of the potential use, and importance, of sport in politics.

What may be called the old Commonwealth sports stayed loyal longest to South Africa; rugby and cricket bodies and teams in particular continued to invite them and to tour there. The ties were undoubtedly strong. In these sports the international world was small and the members formed a close-knit club. The arguments used by rugby and cricket men were those aired for the first time in the 1930s, encouraging the building of sporting bridges between nations by keeping politics and sport apart.

Remarkably, for some years governments tried to remain loyal to their position on the Berlin Olympic issue – they left sporting decisions to sports bodies. But gradually opinions were changing, at least behind the scenes as ministers and officials realised that foreign and other interests were at stake. It was in 1970 that everything changed, when one tour, and one man in particular, caused everyone to question their attitudes and decide where their interests and priorities lay.

Peter Hain was born in Nairobi but brought up in South Africa. His father was an architect who fell out with the government and brought his family to England. In 1966 they settled in London with 16-year-old Peter installed at Emanuel school in Battersea. Within a few years he became involved in the growing South African issue. He had painful memories:

134

'I had black friends as a boy, but we used to get separated when we went to events like soccer matches. My brother and I followed the top side in Pretoria, the Arcadia Shepherds. In 1961 blacks were suddenly banned from even watching white teams play. But some were so keen they shinned up trees overlooking the Caledonian stadium. I recall the screams as police with dogs hauled them down; they were taken away, bleeding and with clothes torn. All to preserve the sanctity of an all-white sporting occasion.'

In the late 1960s the sports boycott of South Africa seemed to be working in soccer and track and field and activists sought to extend it to other sports. In October 1969, the famed Springboks came to England for a rugby tour, with internationals against England, Scotland, Ireland and Wales. For Hain and his student colleagues this was a heaven-sent opportunity. The general aim was to publicise their cause; their specific aim was to 'Stop the 70 Tour' – the South African cricket tour of Britain due to take place, under the auspices of the MCC, the following summer.

The rugby tour in the winter of 1969–70 provided the focus for demonstrations and civil dissent the like of which had not been seen in Britain since the Mosley riots in 1930. Hain recalls: 'I never thought that the MCC would take a decision (on the summer cricket tour) on moral or political grounds. The MCC didn't have a moral view about South Africa. They ran cricket according to cricket's needs and had no wider or moral principles. The only way to make an impact was by direct action.'

Throughout that winter's rugby season, Hain was the spokesman for a student-led series of demonstrations at every ground where the Springboks played. Increasingly, matches were disrupted. TV pictures of the push and shove of the maul in and around grounds, with ugly faces and soon ugly incidents, brought the South African issue to the forefront of both newspaper pages and political minds. Families were divided; political parties were divided; but increasingly everyone had a view and usually a strong one.

135

The man they loved to hate. But Peter Hain did stop the 70 Tour of Britain by the South African cricket team

For Hain the campaign reached its low point in Swansea, South Wales, where feelings in favour of the tour and of the Springboks ran highest. There was fierce fighting between demonstrators and 'stewards' at the ground which resulted in dozens of serious injuries. 'That was very, very shocking,' Hain recalls, 'to be at the head of a campaign that was stirring up such hatred.'

But they did achieve their main objective. Although that Springbok rugby tour was completed, albeit with a high cost in policing and in bruised feelings around the sporting scene, the 1970 cricket tour was cancelled after consultation between the government and the MCC. Direct action had succeeded. The tour had to be cancelled because it would have been impossible to protect and police effectively a number of cricket matches around Britain. Hain remembers his 'sheer relief'; he and his colleagues had wondered how they would maintain their pitch of activity for much longer.

Hain recalls it all as 'a hardening experience' and undoubtedly there were hard feelings all round. The 'keep politics out of sport' banner has waved for some years since. But the new lesson then was that direct action could work and it was soon taken up by the emerging political muscles in black Africa. In 1976 the Montreal Olympic Games were boycotted by 32 countries following another Springbok tour, this time to New Zealand. Now, action was by governments. For black Africa particularly sport was clearly a legitimate and effective weapon to deploy in foreign policy. This meant that the threat of boycott hung for a while over many international sports events. Commonwealth events were a particular target, if only because of the numerical dominance of the black African states within the loose framework of the old British Empire. (South Africa of course had left the Commonwealth in 1961.) Pressure within the Commonealth was applied and felt increasingly at government level and led in 1977 to the first concerted action, the so-called 'Gleneagles agreement'.

The name Gleneagles comes from the hotel in Scotland where the Commonwealth heads of government met for their biannual meeting in 1977. The proper title of the document produced there is 'The Commonwealth Statement on Apartheid in Sport'. Its immediate purpose was to forestall a boycott of the Commonwealth Games due in Edmonton in 1978. Through this agreement, Commonwealth governments agreed to 'discourage sporting contacts' with South Africa while the apartheid system was in place.

The 'Gleneagles agreement' was a landmark because, for the first time, governments were formally committed to play a role in sporting decisions. They were now involved in whether or not matches of any kind were played against South African teams, either at home or away. Small wonder that the 'hands off sport' lobby that was first heard between 1933 and 1936 was so enraged over this agreement. For Conservative politicans in Britain in particular, Gleneagles was a *bête noire* that could be relied upon to spill tea cups at any Party gathering throughout the land. Some sports bodies objected, too, on grounds of their independence. Peter Lawson, the general secretary of the CCPR (Central Council of Physical Recreation) in the UK, argued that: 'This was an agreement between governments and sport was never consulted. But whenever sport bodies sought to build bridges to South Africa through sport, it was used against them.'

In the now frequent debates around the world about politics and sport, old arguments had become entrenched. Peter Hain always believed that the South African case was special. What made it unique 'such that you can't divorce sport from politics, was that it was the only country which infected its entire sports' structure from school through to clubs, through provincial and national organisation, with racism – with discriminatory policies.' Some argued simply that apartheid was a matter for South Africans and that everyone else should mind their own business. Some argued that sport was a way to 'civilise' the apartheid regime. This was the 'building bridges' view advanced in the 1930s and echoed by sports' administrators like Peter Lawson. Mixed teams from other shores might teach South Africans the error of their ways, especially if the Springboks were beaten! The trouble was South Africa did not want mixed teams.

In 1968, the South African government vetoed the choice of Basil D'Oliviera, who had been born in South Africa to a 'Cape Coloured' family, after he had been selected for an England tour by the MCC. The D'Oliviera affair finally put paid to any notion of officially sanctioned sporting links by the MCC and probably did the South African government's case more harm than a hundred demonstrations. But they might have had their hands full of dissent if D'Oliviera had batted the best white bowlers of the day all round the lush green cricket ground at Newlands in Cape Town, almost within hitting distance of the shabby shanty town which confined the young Basil during his childhood.

Talking to Peter Hain now, he feels entirely vindicated by events. 'One of the crosses radical protesters have to bear is that they are not popular at the time. But I was never in the business of striking poses. The objective was to get a nonracial system in South Africa. Even people like Danie Craven (the President of the white South African Rugby Board) 'eventually admitted that our campaign was justified.' But opponents like Peter Lawson are also unrepentant. 'The sad regime had to fall, and who's to say that it would not have happened quicker if sport had been used as a means of communication rather than boycott?'

The pace of reform and change in South Africa has quickened to a dash in the last two years, under the de Klerk administration. Most observers accept that the international sporting boycott has played a significant part in bringing South Africa to such long awaited change. Mike Brearley, formerly England's cricket captain, told the *Daily Mirror* over a decade ago that even then 'any achievements in multi-racial sport over there have been obtained through South Africa being isolated.' The authors of this book are convinced by the argument that sport played a part, even a significant one, in bringing about political change in South Africa. Sport alone could not have done much, but as part of the war, its campaigns have been crucial.

Apartheid is not quite dead yet. But its straitened circumstances can reasonably be traced back to April 1975. The quiet revolution which overthrew a decaying military regime in Portugal began a process which unseated colonial buffers in Angola and Mozambique and eventually Zimbabwe, and left South Africa completely isolated at the tip of the continent. South Africa's growing political isolation coincided with the increasing realisation of the power of sport in politics.

It is a measure of the speed of change that in 1991 Sam Ramsamy became chairman of the newly formed, multi-racial, South African Olympic Committee, sitting with white members of the previous South African Olympic bodies who, until recently, had been his implacable opponents. Ramsamy was formerly head of SANROC (South African Non Racial Olympic Committee) and a passionate fighter to keep his country out of the international sporting arena until apartheid was beaten. Sport can heal as well as hurt, and Ramsamy is hoping Seb Coe and others will now come to South Africa to coach his athletes and players and help the process of normalising and modernising sport within the Republic.

A lot changed in 1991. Peter Hain was one to alter his views: 'It was clear that power was ebbing away from the white sports organisations, and their allies abroad, to the black sports bodies and the ANC. I felt we should set the agenda. We'd had to say no for 20 years. Now, it was the chance to say yes, but it had to be on our terms. Rather than let the whites move in, with their resources and organisation, to bring blacks within their ambit, we should take the initiative.'

The sheer pace of change is exhilarating. Maybe, some healthy competition helped – between the IOC and the IAAF. Although both bodies deny it, both seemed keen in 1991 to be the first to get South Africa back into international sport. Perhaps the key initiative came from President Samaranch of the IOC, who asked Sam Ramsamy to lead an Olympic commission to assess changes and events in South Africa. The favourable report led to a similar visit from an IAAF committee, which recommended that South Africa could be readmitted to international track and field. There was even some frustration at the slowness of bodies and people in South Africa to make the necessary organisational changes. Jean-Claude Ganga, the IOC member from Congo, said in June 1991: 'We are like a train standing at the station. We cannot wait if people do not get on.' Not very long before, Ganga had been one of the most vociferous supporters of the boycott.

In July came the momentous decision to invite South Africa back into the Olympic fold. We asked Sam Ramsamy what factors finally precipitated this speedy process of change, after more than thirty years of sporting isolation. He told us: 'It was the final abolition of most of the apartheid laws which motivated the international community and sports movement to reconsider their attitude towards South African sport.' He argues that the IOC and the African sports movement provided the vital, timely leadership in the rethink of the boycott, which 'was undoubtedly responsible for highlighting the issue of apartheid internationally'.

140

The sporting boycott of South Africa kept many fine sportsmen and women (black and white) out of international competition. Marcel Winkler is one of those now tipped for stardom

141

Governments have become increasingly sophisticated in their use of the sporting weapon, to achieve goals, to strike useful political postures in the world or at home. Between 1963 and 1966, the then British Prime Minister, Harold Wilson, gave resources and help to the preparations for the 1966 World Cup in England because he recognised the Berlin lessons of prestige and propaganda. In 1971 President Nixon used 'ping pong diplomacy' to open up links and trade relations with China. It was the first time an official delegation of Americans (the ping pong team) had entered mainland China in almost 20 years. In 1973 the French government cancelled an Australian sport tour because of local objections to their nuclear tests in the Pacific. In 1976 there was a lengthy and difficult dispute between China, Taiwan and the IOC, about Taiwan's eligibility for the Olympic Games. In 1977 there was 'basketball diplomacy' between the USA and Cuba. In an indirect attempt to lift the US trade embargo against Cuba, Senator George McGovern took the two South Dakota state university basketball teams to Cuba, where they both lost to the Cuban national team. In 1988 the Olympic movement came within a cycling circuit of uniting North and South Korea, at least for the period of the Seoul Olympics. The plan was to site some of the Games' events in North Korea. But agreement could not be reached. When Seoul was awarded the Olympics in 1981, South Korea had no formal diplomatic relations with 44 of the Olympic nations. Following the Games, they re-established relations with many of the participating countries, including, for example, Hungary, China and the USSR.

The Olympic Games has always been a focus for national tensions and tempers, because it is the premier contest in world sport. But the fierceness of one 'sporting' encounter was an accident of timing. On December 6, 1956, in Melbourne Australia, Hungary met the USSR in the semi-final of the Olympic water polo tournament. Just four weeks before 200 000 Soviet troops had invaded Hungary to suppress a

142

revolution against Communist rule, and in the bloody resistance 7000 Hungarians lost their lives. With that background, it was never going to be an ordinary polo match. Before loud and partisan support, the Hungarians played out of their skins and polo caps, but it was literally a fight all the way; the referee had to abandon the game just before the end, with Hungary leading 4–0, or there would have been a riot. Blood was in the water, and the following day newspapers carried a striking picture of the Hungarian Ervin Zador with a blood stained face. The symbolism was not lost on 10 million Hungarians who had just lost their country to the Soviet bear.

The Soviet invasion of Afghanistan in 1979 never fired European or American opinion as highly as the attack on Hungary in 1956, or of Czechoslovakia in 1968. But it nearly brought the Olympic movement to its knees.

Two of the authors of this book were involved in the Olympic Games in Moscow in 1980; Seb Coe as one of the star athletes and David Wickham as a BBC producer on the spot, covering not the sport, but the politics. Unlike many others journalists had long realised that sport and politics were inseparable. Western governments wanted to express their strong disapproval of the Soviet invasion but were not prepared to take military action. This was still Cold War politics. President Carter looked around for ways to pursue American interests and found (as Hitler did half a century earlier) that just at hand was an Olympic host city. This time, it was not in his own country, but in the Soviet Union itself. What better way to damage his Russian opponent without endangering American lives (or economic interests) than to use the boycott weapon; a tactical weapon, about whose range and accuracy so much was now known from the experiences of the previous two decades. The President called in American sports chiefs and told them it was not possible to separate an American team abroad from American interests. In the current climate between his government and that of the USSR it would not be appropriate to send an American team to Moscow. He ordered them not to go.

143

President Carter turned next to his allies. In Britain the Prime Minister was Margaret Thatcher, elected just the year before, and not known for 'politicking' in sport. Indeed, the Conservative party had opposed the 'Gleneagles agreement' as 'state interference' and vowed to repeal it (which they soon found difficult, as any change required the agreement of Commonwealth heads of state, many of whom were strongly attached to the document). Peter Hain writing much later noted wryly these two statements by the Thatcher family:

'We are a free people playing an amateur game and we have got the right to play where we like ... as sure as hell we can play our game in South Africa'

(Dennis Thatcher, to London Society of Rugby Football Referees, December 1979), and:

'British athletes have the same rights and the same responsibilities towards freedom and its maintenance as every citizen of the UK ... for British athletes to take part in the Games in Moscow ... would be for them to seem to condone an international crime'

(Margaret Thatcher, letter to Chairman of the BOA, 19 February 1980).

Peter Hain supported the US and British governments in the Moscow boycott, whilst noting: 'it was striking how abruptly those political figures, who for decades had criticised opponents of white South African participation in international sport, suddenly discovered the abiding virtues of mixing politics and sport ... their conversion was quite moving.' Hain saw this boycott as very much 'a tactical weapon. There was nothing especially principled about it.'

Mrs Thatcher tried to steer a middle course – something else that was foreign to her nature. Although she followed the spirit of the Gleneagles' example and discouraged her country's sportsmen and women from participating in Moscow, she did not match President Carter's outright ban. The reaction, as we have already noted, was mixed. Some

144

athletes went to the Games, some did not. The BOA displayed a care and fortitude that put its 1936 forebears to shame, although its final decision was still to support the movement. The then Chairman, Sir Dennis Follows, had to face the forceful arguments of Margaret Thatcher herself and much of the establishment, but he stayed patient and firm. The BOA would go, because it believed the Games should not be used as a tactical device in the Cold War. This time, there were no racist issues, in the BOA's view. They were aware of the treatment of Jews in the Soviet Union, but that was not the reason why the government was asking them not to go.

Peter Lawson was also involved in the debate within British sport, and with the Thatcher government, and he believed strongly that the BOA's stance was right. He recalls that the meeting of the Central Council of Physical Recreation to discuss the issue brought one of the largest attendances in memory. 'First, we considered this was a decision for sport. But if the government had said to us "Look, we have decided not to trade any more with the USSR because of this issue of principle", then we'd have felt we were part of a unified, consistent national policy. But we couldn't avoid the feeling that sport was being picked off as a cheap option.'

The Thatcher government united some people both on the right and on the left of the political spectrum, but not everyone, and similarly people and politicans of all persuasions also supported the stance of the BOA. Seb Coe recalls how difficult the decision over Moscow was for him personally: 'I have always been a political animal and of course believed in the fusion of sport and politics. With Moscow my sporting and political views coincided. I thought the Games were an important event that sportspeople should support; and I didn't think a boycott would have the necessary impact on Soviet policy. People made comparisons with South Africa, but that was so different. We knew that boycott was effective. And my sport's governing bodies began and supported the South African boycott, whereas they all encouraged me to go to Moscow.'

145

In a sense, both sides were right, and both won the day. The Games went on, in all their splendour, but nothing could conceal the international opprobrium over the invasion of Afghanistan, or even over the events at home. The boycott was widely reported; the absence from the Games of some great sportspeople was an everyday reminder of the political context. By contrast, two years before, in staging the World Cup Argentina had managed to conceal that country's sub-human policy of 'disappearing' its opponents. The spectacle in the stadiums spoke of a civilised nation having a wonderful time. Not so in Moscow – the show of plenty put on for visitors was seen through. David Wickham recalls that the hotels for visitors were filled to bursting point with food while the rest of the city, and perhaps the whole countryside, was stripped of fresh vegetables. 'I remember tucking into a delicious tomato and dill salad at dinner one evening in the house of some Russian friends; the conversation turned to tomatoes and I remarked on the mountains of them I had passed on my way into breakfast that morning at the newly built Cosmos hotel, where all the television journalists were staying. There was an embarrassed silence and it later transpired that our hostess had queued for over four hours to buy these tomatoes!' As in Berlin, the overriding requirement of the Moscow Games was to leave a good impression on the visiting foreigners. For this purpose the city was cleared of known dissidents and refuseniks who might attract unfavourable attention from the visiting foreign press; many were exiled from Moscow just for the duration of the 22nd Olympiad. Did the boycott have any real effect on the Russian people themselves? The answer has to be no; on its own, sport hasn't got that power. It is only when combined with economic and other forces over a period, that sport becomes a powerful weapon for change and for reform.

Were any women among the authors of this book they might argue that sport is not a powerful enough weapon for either change or reform; sport's record on equal status for women is badly blemished. Women were not admitted into

Not allowed to compete. For most of the century, women were barred from running an Olympic marathon. America's Joan Benoit was the first winner when the event was finally allowed in 1984. Here she breaks the world record, in Boston, Massachusetts a year before

track and field at the modern Olympic Games until 1928 and even then only for restricted events – just the 100 metres, 800 metres, high jump and discus. The first 'distance' event permitted to them was the 1500 metres in 1972, and women were only allowed to run an Olympic marathon in 1984. This

was prejudice of the flat earth kind. Now, experts like Dr Craig Sharp (Director of Physiology at the British Olympic medical centre) accept that women are better equipped for endurance events than men because they can hold fluid better and use body fat more efficiently. He said in July 1991: 'Had Scott of the Antarctic been a woman, he might have made it!' He also argued that the 1991 world 10 000 metre champion, Liz McColgan, benefited greatly from bearing a child nine month before: 'Pregnancy is an anabolic event,' he told *The Times*. Nevertheless, even now many events like the pole-vault, steeplechase and triple jump are for men only. And sometimes even when accepted, women have had to endure queries about their sexuality, a tribute to man's continuing discomfort with the notion of women athletes. In 1936 Helen Stephens of America was the female equivalent of Jesse Owens. After she beat the Polish favourite Stanislawa Walasiewic to win the women's 100 metres, Poland doubted her talent and obliged the authorities to conduct a sex test. Stephens was judged to be a woman. Ironically Walasiewic was found to have male sex organs when the subject of an autopsy 44 years later after a motoring accident in the USA.

Women now play most of the major sports and are attempting breakthroughs in male preserves like rugby, baseball, soccer and the martial arts. But women are still represented by different organisations for most sports in most countries. Oases of prejudice remain in all-male sports clubs. Top British soccer clubs still protect the sanctity of their boardrooms from the dreaded scent and sound of women. Exceptions had to be made for Prime Minister Margaret Thatcher, in the mid-1980s, or there might have been a real crisis in certain clubs. One of the leading civil servants on sport and football during the 80s was a woman, Jan Anderson, and she found herself all too often separated from her male colleagues at matches.

On the whole, sport has a better record with disabled people than with women. There are opportunities and events which make a real contribution to the quality of life of many disabled people. But there remain exceptions which tarnish the image.

The disabled Olympics continue to be separated from the main Games, and do not actually carry the Olympic imprimatur. Access to many stadiums around the world is no better and often worse than access to other theatres of entertainment.

Simon Barnes of *The Times* remarked (June 1991) that: 'Sport and politics are ever blood brothers.' The sheer growth of sport, as a business, and its media impact, mean that politicians have to take it seriously. Sport is now a major employer and a significant part of most economies. Its big events are the biggest now staged in the world. Its heroes and heroines are similarly giant-like. Its problems also tend to be big, and often international, often requiring governmental help, advice, direction and intervention.

But one prejudice of the 1930s remains in what C.P. Snow called the 'corridors of power'. To the career politician or civil servant, whether in Europe or the USA, sport is not a heavyweight subject. It does not sit at the Cabinet table, or in the Oval Office. It does not tilt elections. It does not make political careers. In Britain some have whispered that the job of Sports Minister is a way to end them. The title is only a courtesy title and it carries the most junior ministerial rank. Only in the USSR and in the old East Germany has the government's sports post been of the first rank. In those cases, it denotes of course the priority given by the states concerned to developing national sport for the prestige and trade that can be won. Those benefits are recognised in most countries, but politicians believe either that they are not of sufficient weight to justify full ministerial responsibility, or still retain doubts about whether or not it is proper for the state to take a leading role in sport.

When David Teasdale left his sports portfolio in Whitehall to work on housing policy issues, one minister remarked: 'You have got a real job at last.' Sport still lingers on the back pages of political life, despite Berlin, Mexico, Montreal, Moscow, Gleneagles, and the talk and turmoil of the African continent. It must campaign to hit the front.

9 Sport in a box

We have now reached a stage where sport at top level has become almost completely show business with everything that one associates with show biz; the cult of the individual, high salaries, the desire to present a game as a spectacle – with more money, less sports-manship, more emphasis on winning. All this has come about through television

SIR DENNIS FOLLOWS, CHAIRMAN OF THE BRITISH OLYMPIC
ASSOCIATION, 1983

It's Zurich, August 1981, the day of that highlight of the track and field Grand Prix in Europe, the Weltklasse meeting. Sebastian Coe is the reigning Olympic 1500 metres champion and he has already broken two world records that summer. He's sitting quietly in the home of his friend, Andreas Brugger, the meeting's promoter, counting down to his attempt that evening on the world mile record held by Steve Ovett. The phone rings. It's the BBC, from London; a senior news executive informs Coe that the Corporation intends to break into their flagship, the news at 9 o'clock, for a live event – his race. Coe listens, with due respect. At the end of the call, the executive didn't wish him good luck. He said, simply and with careful purpose: 'So I hope you're aware that this is important to us.'

Coe did break the world record. He has sometimes wondered since if he might have saved somebody's job that night. Today, the media interest in sport and sports people is intense. A quite modest event might attract hundreds of journalists and cameramen, who have privileged status and positions. And as public interest grows, the status of, and facilities for, the press both get better. The great Test cricket ground at Headingley followed other stadia in 1991 in opening

The press at work at the Seoul Olympics, 1988. At the Barcelona Olympic Games in 1992 there will be more media than competitors

new press facilities, perfectly sited behind the bowler's arm. A modern Olympic Games has to provide a separate village for about 10 000 representatives of the world's media. At any sports event, an extra piece of live entertainment is the gaggle of cameras and scribes around a star performer – especially if there is some controversy in the air.

The pressure for copy, for the exclusive picture or comment, can be intrusive and intense and some sports stars have found it stifling as media stars. Some even retire early as a result, depriving sports' fans of the pleasure of watching them. Barry John quit rugby early; George Best left soccer; and the best behaved tennis champion of recent years, Bjorn Borg, quit his game under this sort of pressure. Sport was the poorer for the departure of all three, and there are plenty of other examples.

Judge Earl Warren, once Governor of California, said: 'the sports page records people's accomplishments – the front page has nothing but man's failures.' Time was when sports coverage was 'straight'; when news and personal items about individuals and teams were very much the exception, rather than the rule. Now, we have the *National Enquirer* and its tabloid ilk in other countries probing the private lives of players.

Some, like Steve Ovett, get angry: 'I hate this attitude the media have that just because someone is good at sport means that their opinion on any subject is of fantastic importance.' Television professionals like Ross Greenberg of the American cable television network, HBO, defend the media's interest in players as people: 'If you don't know (them) then you don't know what's behind their ... event, or the athletic prowess in that individual sport. What we have to do is inform ... and then you can live and breathe with those people's ups and downs *and* their careers.'

Sport has always been worth reporting. It provides drama, both tense and exciting; there are winners and losers, pain, laughter and tragedy. It is uncertain, often to the finish, and it is intensely human. It makes headlines, it makes a good read, it makes pictures. Maurice Yaffe, the sports psychologist, observed that 'the sport arena is a wonderful laboratory for observation.' From the earliest days there were observers who spread the word about the happenings in the arena. Greek and Roman writers and poets recorded many sporting contests. In the *Iliad*, Homer recorded in some detail the games organised at the funeral of Patroclus.

The popularity of sport in Victorian and Edwardian England gave rise to a number of sporting papers. *Bell's Life in London*, founded in 1922, was perhaps the first. Originally a news sheet it reported increasingly on horse racing and prize fighting. There was also the *Sporting Magazine* which concentrated mainly on hunting, and the *Sporting Life*, which did the same for racing and had a circulation of 300 000 by the 1880s. The *Athletic News* was established in 1875 to report football, and soon claimed a circulation of 100 000. These were high figures for a period when England's total population was only approximately 22 million and probably only half of those could read and write. In the Britain of the early 1900s, almost every town and city had its own *Sports Special*, a Saturday night newspaper or news sheet reporting the sporting results and events of local teams that day. Richard Holt reports in *Sport and the British: A Modern History* that 'from the 1920s sports reporting and photography was accepted as a crucial and specialised component of popular journalism.'

In America sport was increasingly featured first in the *American Farmer* from 1819 and then in other news sheets, including the *Spirit of the Times* from 1831.

Throughout the twentieth century, there has been a growing band of sports reporters. For a sports fan they led a charmed life, watching events and then reporting what happened.

Then there was radio. Its microphones 'were there' with the reporters. Through them we were able to hear what was happening, as it happened. Sport was a major part of radio programmes and of radio's development. Millions got up in the night in Britain to hear Test matches from Australia; millions stayed up on America's eastern seaboard to hear baseball games from California.

153

Catch old broadcasters on a good evening and they will invariably regale you with wonderful stories of the golden days of radio. It was live action on the air, at the turn of a dial, and the listener depended absolutely and entirely upon the 'Man with the Mike'; his description fed one's imagination, sitting in domestic comfort, or in a bar or office. One of the best British broadcasters was Raymond Glendenning but even he could sometimes miss a piece of the action. The tale is told that he once looked away just as a goal was scored. There was no need to admit to a mistake – he simply carried on and reported the goal a minute or so later. The listener was not there and never knew.

To help the listener's imagination, visual data was sometimes given via magazines, or newspapers. In 1927 the BBC's *Radio Times* made a famous attempt at greater efficiency in soccer broadcasting. They printed a diagram of the soccer field divided into marked squares. The idea was that the commentator would inform listeners as the play moved between these squares, so that they were better able to keep up with the flow of the game. The experiment was short lived!

Then came television, and again, sport played an important part in its growth. Now we could see the action as it happened – if not yet when it happened. We saw how goals and runs were scored and precisely how the contender was knocked out. For the first time, we too 'were there'.

In the mid-1930s, Britain, Germany and America were racing to be the first with TV pictures. At the Berlin Olympics in 1936, TV cameras and screens with very fuzzy pictures were the objects of curious interest. But probably the first real outside broadcast was by the BBC, in 1937, and it was 25 minutes of a men's singles match from Wimbledon. Only a few hundred Londoners could see it; the television service was still experimental. Shortly before, CBS had attempted, without real success, to broadcast a fight by 'sight and sound'. Both the American and British realised that boxing, with its small restricted ring of activity, was suited to the inflexible

Back to square one. With the BBC's *Radio Times* diagram of the 1927 Cup Final pitch at Wembley, the commentators could plot the play for listeners

APRIL 15, 1927.] — RADIO TIMES — 129

Broadcasting the Match of the Year.

THIS afternoon—Saturday, April 23—the broadcasting of sporting events will reach another landmark in its history. Listeners all over the country will be able to hear in their own homes the story, told from the ground during the actual progress of the game, of the match that packs the biggest arena in the country every year, on an occasion that is the red-letter day in the calendar of everyone who follows the national winter game.

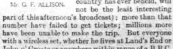

Mr. G. F. ALLISON.

There will be 100,000 people in the Wembley Stadium (and to hear this vast crowd singing together before the kick-off, the largest demonstration of Community Singing this country has ever beheld, will not be the least interesting part of this afternoon's broadcast); more than that number have failed to get tickets; millions more have been unable to make the trip. But everyone with a wireless set, whether he lives at Land's End or John o' Groats or anywhere within range of a B.B.C.

station, will be in all the of those days history is The actual promises to be as any ever The two Allison and whose pictures have been remany previous tives, and the occasion have them. The for transmission are unusually simple and compact. The portable sound-proof hut, which is becoming a familiar sight to match-goers, will at Wembley be situated at the right-hand end of the Press Gallery, which commands an unrivalled view of the field. There will be two microphones in the hut, and the control point for the engineers will be immediately behind, between the hut and the back wall of the Press Gallery. Thence two pairs of private lines run direct to Savoy Hill, where the messages will be dealt with in the ordinary way.

THE CAUSE OF THE TROUBLE.

able to share thrills of one when football made.

broadcast as successful carried out. narrators, Mr. Mr. McCulloch, you see inset, sponsible for football narrathrills of a big no terrors for arrangements

The broadcast, then, promises to be—like the Boat Race narrative—a worthy account of the match. And what a match it will be! Both teams have fine records in the earlier stages of the tournament, and won their way to Wembley by decisive victories against formidable opposition. Each has had to replay one match, and won the replay at home. Both play in the First Division of the League, where they are of almost equal standing; at the time of writing only one point separates them. All London will be backing the Arsenal, and Wales will be solid behind Cardiff City. No element of excitement seems to have been left out.

Mr. D. McCULLOCH

First the Rugby Internationals; then the Grand National and the Boat Race; and now the Cup Final. Is it too much to claim that broadcasting has become as important to followers of sport as it has long been to music-lovers and to people who want to dance?

This is the Wembley Stadium, packed with a cheering crowd of 100,000 people, as it will appear this afternoon when The Arsenal and Cardiff City are fighting for the Cup. The B.B.C. narrators will be at the top of the covered stand in the left-hand corner of the picture—just beside the domed tower in the foreground—and the sections numbered on the field are those that they will use in describing the course of the greatest game of the year.

demands of the new apparatus. In 1939 both BBC and NBC broadcast fights. That year BBC also showed its first FA Cup Final and NBC its first baseball.

After the War, TV still had a very small audience, but on both sides of the Atlantic broadcasters continued to cover sport with increasing interest and success. By 1956, 75 per cent of American households had TV sets but in Britain the figure was still much lower. Still television launched a golden age for sport, and of course it brought some problems of its own. John Bromley, one of the old breed of sports reporters in Britain working on the *Daily Mirror*, was recruited for TV early on in this new age. He joined ITV in 1964, when, he recalls, 'the new network was trying to mount a serious challenge to the BBC, who were dominant in sport. They'd had a huge head start through radio and just carried on into

Who's watching who? Arsenal footballers break off training at Highbury Stadium, north London, to inspect an early outside broadcast TV camera

156

TV.' He became ITV's Head of Sport for many years, a familiar figure around the sport and broadcasting centres of the world. Bromley recalls clearly, and with affection, those early days: 'The game then was chasing audiences. Sport pulled big audiences. But the BBC had the main domestic events tied up. They also had three great advantages – their experienced professionalism, a loyal audience and they had no commercial breaks.'

Peter Dimmock, then the Head of BBC Sport, had cemented the Corporation's position with an earlier coup. He persuaded the government that there was a danger that the great and popular British sporting events like the soccer Cup Final, cricket Test matches, the Grand National and the British Grand Prix might be lost to public viewing if they were allowed to be bought by the new commercial station, Independent Television (ITV), then operating only in the London area. The government passed a law specifying listed sporting events which had to be broadcast nationwide because of their public appeal. Potentially, this was government interfering in sport and in a free press and media, but they got away with it! Dimmock, now retired, told us that the original government decision was a 'common-sense one; but it always surprised me that this list ... remained in being for so long once its original purpose was satisfied. It always puzzled me once ITV became nationwide that the organisers of such events as the FA Cup Final and the Grand National did not press hard for its abolition to obtain higher TV rights fees on an exclusive basis.' He also described it as 'quite extraordinary' that the government should at last propose to abolish the list in 1991, after some 35 years, when there was the same original danger that a new minority channel – this time, a satellite or cable network – might purchase one of these events and thus restrict their viewing to an even smaller proportion of the population.

John Bromley and ITV began their sports magazine programme *World of Sport* headed by Eamonn Andrews in 1965. Initially, there were some shared events with the BBC (including Wimbledon) but the BBC always put competition

157

before co-operation. The BBC had the best domestic events sewn up, and ITV were forced to look elsewhere in the world for their coverage. Bromley told us: 'I got on aeroplanes and found sport. Bits from the USA, from Spain, many different places. We were like two shops side by side in the high street. One had all the British goods. We had to say "Come and look at this." We found amazing things like cliff diving in Acapulco. There was a lot of boxing, of course. And we established one regular, winning slot with wrestling. It was much criticised but it lasted 30 years as TV entertainment, with six million people watching.'

Similar magazine programmes were established in the USA. ABC had *Wide World of Sport*, NBC had *Sportsworld* and CBS had *Sports Spectacular*. All chased the huge audience potential of sport. For many years all provided taped programmes; but, as Bromley observed: 'it was the demand for live sport in the last few years that hastened the end of these programmes.'

Show business has never been far from television, and never more so than when the impresario Lew Grade presided at ITV. John Bromley recalls one story: an executive rushed into his office to report excitedly that ITV had won coverage of athletic events from the BBC; there was an agreement with the 'Three As'. Grade enquired, who were the 'Three As'? The Amateur Athletic Association, he was told. Grade exploded: 'How many times do I have to tell you, we don't want any bloody amateurs here!'

Such was the competition to feed the growing audience that more than anywhere else, TV sport was pushing constantly at the boundaries of technology. Smaller and more flexible cameras, multi-camera outside broadcast facilities and split screen pictures were all developed for sport. Satellite coverage first came to the fore for major sports events. It was no coincidence that in both radio and television at the BBC for a time, the Head of Sport was also the Head of Outside Broadcasts and looked after the grand State occasions. The sports department was the major user of television's new toys.

The slow motion replay was developed for sport; 'The first machine in 1968 cost us £60 000 ($144 000), then a colossal sum,' John Bromley recalls, 'but it brought in results.' When the BBC news department, who usually had most of their own facilities, first used slow-motion to highlight a sequence they had to go to the sports department.

Sports television technology continues to evolve. In a first for British technology, live interviews from the Rothmans yacht in the Fastnet race in August 1991 were transmitted to television. Previously, television producers had to rely on secondhand reports or crew videos turned in at port to monitor the progress of the race during the weeks that the yachts were at sea. Developed by British Telecom, the technology is a prototype of the ocean-going system that will be carried by several of the yachts entered for the 1993/4 Whitbread Round the World Race. Besides the live interviews, edited highlights of life on board and of the race itself can be compressed and

Some day every boat will be like this! A specially designed satellite transmitter sends live TV pictures from the Rothmans yacht during the 1991 Fastnet race

then stored electronically prior to television transmission. A specially designed transmitter on the back of the yacht sends the pictures via satellite to the television station. From there the pictures can be transmitted around the world; mid-ocean dramas played out live in our living rooms.

The story of sport and the media had to be rewritten with the advent of TV. These are two parts of what one might call an 'unholy trinity'. The third part is sponsorship. In the last 30 years, around the world, these three – sport, sponsors and TV – have stayed close and grown together.

The advent of the trinity represented a sea change in the history and development of sport. TV did not invent sports stars, there had been plenty before; and it did not invent sponsors and product endorsements, which were already busy in sport. But TV has pushed the Star Trek Enterprise machine into hyperspace. Philippe Chatrier said on his retirement as President of the ITF (International Tennis Federation): 'You know our game looks so good on television, it brings in masses of money and sponsors and everything.' And Ross Greenberg of HBO told us that 'television has brought dollar signs to sports more than anything else.'

And it is money that links the trinity. In truth, the three have nothing else in common, although there are often fine words from business and TV executives about their objectives. Essentially both have a business deal with sport. The trinity is a loose financial conglomerate. But who's in charge? Who calls the TV shots?

In principle, sport should be in charge, but the income from TV and sponsors has become so important that sometimes it isn't. In 1986, the soccer World Cup was played in Mexico. The highest sums for TV coverage were paid by European TV stations, but they wanted to show games in Europe in the evenings to maximise their audiences and thus their returns. That meant playing matches in the heat of the middle of the day, the worst time for the players – ironically, especially those from Europe. That is what TV wanted, so that is what happened.

(*Left*) Armed with the ball: Michael Jordan of the Chicago Bulls in the 1991 NBA play-offs against the Los Angeles Lakers
(*Stephen Dunn/Allsport*)

(*Overleaf*) High dawn on Mount Arapiles in Victoria, Australia
(*Brian Bailey/Allsport*)

(*Below*) Beating the ball: The Royals against the Bluejays, 1991
(*Rick Stewart/Allsport*)

Walking on water: a
disabled athlete in an
everyday miracle
(*Oli Tennent/Allsport*)

Making waves: powerboat
racing at Nice in 1990, with
Pedrini and her British crew
(*Bob Martin/Allsport*)

20/20 vision: golfer supreme Jack Nicklaus 'sees' every shot in his mind's eye before he plays it
(*David Cannon/Allsport*)

(*Left*) Tight corners: Switzerland's Vreni Schneider was world champion at giant slalom in 1987, and at slalom and giant slalom again in 1989
(*David Cannon/Allsport*)

(*Below left*) Katarina Witt, German superstar of ice dancing, pictured in Paris in 1987
(*Vandystadt/Allsport, France*)

(*Right*) Gold medal mother: Liz McColgan of Britain became the 10 000 metres world champion and a mother in 1991. Here she beats Susan Sirma of Kenya in the Grand Prix meeting at Zurich in the same year
(*Bob Martin/Allsport*)

(*Below*) First among equals: now running for a united Germany, the former East German star Katrina Krabbe wins the 1991 World Championships 100 metres from the hot favourite Merlene Ottey (Jamaica) and Gwen Torrance (USA)
(*Billy Stickland/Allsport*)

Fair play on the field: Gary Lineker helping Tottenham Hotspur to win the 1991 FA Cup Final against Nottingham Forest (*Shaun Botterill/Allsport*)

In the last 10 to 15 years some of the world's best track and field events have been staged in Europe. A prime audience is in America, whose TV networks compete with each other and therefore pay the highest fees. The time difference has meant that promoters have often pushed their key events back into the very late evening. This has not suited every athlete's body clock. Seb Coe was lucky, and liked running late. But Steve Ovett often complained. Seb says of Steve: 'I remember he used to bring an alarm clock on to the track with him as his form of protest'!

Sometimes the pressure by television companies to change the start times of events can backfire. Alex Gillardi of the American NBC network surmises that the television audience of the Seoul Olympic Games in 1988 may have been *reduced* by start times which did not suit the live audience: 'The live events ... happened early in the morning, 9.30, but people were not in the stands yet. In America they thought if people have not bothered to sit and watch this event, maybe it's not important enough.'

In American football, TV is the paymaster and it calls a number of the shots. Steven Barnett, in his book *Games and Sets*, reports that in 1951 the entire NFL earned only $50 000 (£18 000) from TV. In 1955 an experimental interruption in play was introduced; referees could call a time-out (a break in play) in the first and third quarters, without request from the teams. 'It was a rule change that convinced advertisers that football was serious about TV,' says Barnett, 'from then on, TV was increasingly serious about football.' The unscheduled pause became institutionalised as a 'TV time-out'. Nowadays, American football is totally geared to television's needs and schedules. TV floor managers even cue the umpires. Depending on the location of key games (eg East or West coast), kick off times are decided in effect by the networks. Changes have also been made in the rules of the game to make it more 'offensive', for example, the extra protection for the quarterbacks and receivers introduced in 1977.

The impact of this relationship on the flow of the game –

161

and perhaps its character – causes concern in America, and some people question the TV/sport relationship. Some concerns come from television itself. Donald Colantonio of ESPN argues that TV companies 'shouldn't be in a position where we affect what's happening on the playing field.' But he stresses that TV 'is the bread and butter of sport,' and in return for their money, television requires something from the sports organisers. 'We're pumping a lot of money into production costs. Because of that there are certain considerations that we would expect.'

But what sort of considerations? We were interviewing Colantonio at Aspen, Colorado, where ESPN were covering the skiing. 'It's an expensive sport to cover, and if there are weather or technical problems television might request a course hold. We expect that to be granted or considered,' he said. Steve Bornstein, also of ESPN, summed it all up like this: 'I don't think (the skiers) should race at midnight for us under lights, or under circumstances that would put them at jeopardy, but reasonable delays and accomodations are something I would expect from any professional sports franchise.' Colantonio describes the process as: 'A food chain – TV feeds the sponsors and sponsors feed the event organisers.'

Problems come when television's demands cannot be accommodated. The 1994 soccer World Cup will be staged in America and the US networks are concerned that the traditional 90-minute matches in two 45-minute halves do not permit their 8 to 10 minutes per hour commercial break schedule. One idea mooted is to split the match into four periods. Bornstein says: 'I would prefer to keep all sports pure, but the fact of the matter is that, depending on how much you have at risk to televise the match depends on how much you need to modify the sport, to accommodate the messages. That's how the business is based.' Bigger goals for the tournament were also suggested, but having toyed with the idea, FIFA appear to have rejected it.

Other sports have tried to change their game to interest television; squash is one. Bob Morris, chief executive of the

Despite glass-walled courts and other high tech changes squash has not had the impact on TV audiences that its organisers had hoped for

Squash Racquets Association in Britain, told us how they had tried to resolve TV's technical objections: 'first, they said we had to provide a transparent court, so that spectators and TV could see the game. Then, they said the camera could not follow the speed of the ball. When we had dealt with both these points, they told us we should change the scoring system and rules. The French tried that, but still did not get TV coverage.' At the BBC, deputy Head of Sport John Rowlinson's view is that 'the technical issue remains, because it is still hard to follow the ball. But also the rallies are long and the score tends to move too slowly for a broad TV audience.' Morris agrees that viewers are often confused with squash, unless they know the game: 'They see Jahangir Khan win the point after a 50-stroke rally and they wonder what he did that was better. They don't see a clear pattern.' Squash's search goes on. One day perhaps a personality will come on the scene and make such an impact that television will be forced to put squash in their schedules.

Women's sports are also a victim of modern TV times. It is ironic that the media talks often of sex appeal (meaning women's sex appeal) but tends to ignore the potential appeal of women in sport. Women's rugby is a fast growing game, and staged its first World Cup in Wales in 1991. We talked to some of the players in Cardiff during the tournament. They told us their aim is 'to raise the profile of the game … everytime we get press coverage and radio and TV it helps a great deal.' The sport remains 'amateur' in a men's market. One England player lamented that 'it's so hard to raise money for women's sport … We can't always get signed up television coverage for the event.' Maybe they need a personality too.

John Rowlinson stresses how TV's decisions are often influenced by personalities in sport: 'With snooker, it helped that there were characters like Alex Higgins around. Recently, tennis audiences are going down, apart from Wimbledon, and golf's are going up, and the reason must be the different success rate of British players (in the two sports) that people in the UK want to see and follow.'

TV also makes or helps personalities; through them it also affects and shapes behaviour. The media's thirst for drama and excitement can lead some performers to play more to the enlarged gallery. The extra pressure of TV and the rush for results can lead to excesses in behaviour – bad for the image of the sport, but, regrettably, good for TV. Sporting behaviour is now transmitted fast and wide. Schoolboys ape their heroes as they always did, but now they have more opportunity to see and copy them, warts and all. Thus, John McEnroe's disputational style with tennis umpires was soon to be seen on junior courts. Similarly, the clash of elbows round the athletics track now happens at school and college.

Television brings benefits to sport too, enhancing participation – regionally, nationally, across the world. Its impact can have surprising effects. In the once cricket-mad West Indies the televising of American basketball has inspired tremendous interest. Nowadays, youngsters are increasingly pushing soft balls into baskets instead of propelling hard ones against trees.

Certain sports have benefited from TV more than others. In 1972 for example, a waif-like Russian girl named Olga Korbut caught the breath and imagination of millions and transformed gymnastics from nasty memories of physical exercises at school into a major sports entertainment. TV set fire to a game called snooker, confined previously to darkened, dingy rooms. In 1985, 18 million people in Britain stayed up after midnight to watch the world snooker final won by Dennis Taylor (over Steve Davis) on the last black ball of the last frame. TV has brought riches into the coffers of the IOC, IAAF and FIFA and many other sports bodies and helped to spread every sport it has touched. Without TV, would a soccer World Cup ever have brought the game to America? Would the conservative administrators in Britain ever have permitted Sunday matches? Without TV, would the athletic world championships ever have been born? TV has fostered the development and growth of snooker, darts, show jumping and some of the big team sports like American football and soccer.

164

It has also encouraged particular forms of games, like one-day cricket and seven-a-side rugby.

Some of its changes are welcomed by the administrators but not necessarily by everyone else. A man named Van Allen developed the tennis 'tie break', to bring overlong matches into line with television schedules. He died in 1991, just a day before the Wimbledon favourite, Stefan Edberg, lost three successive tie breaks in the semi-final and thus became the first to go out of a major tournament without losing his serve.

But most of all, TV's power has boosted events, and even the Olympics, the biggest of all, was revitalised, perhaps even reborn, in 1984 by Peter Ueberroth's unique perception of TV's latent power and profit. As the architect of the LA Games he firstly negotiated a good deal with the American television networks, stressing 'home advantage' and the huge potential audience. Second – and this was his crucial innovation – he used the TV base to sell different parts of the Olympic package for the first time to sponsors. Now TV and its income are vital in event planning. The table below, from Steven Barnett's *Games and Sets*, illustrates how the value of US television rights for the summer Olympic Games has risen in the last 30 years. (Two thirds of the host city's revenue from the summer Games now comes from the sale of these American rights.)

Year	Venue	Price ($ millions)
1960	Rome	0.394 (£140 000)
1964	Tokyo	1.5
1968	Mexico	4.5
1972	Munich	7.5
1976	Montreal	25
1980	Moscow	85
1984	Los Angeles	225
1988	Seoul	300
1992	Barcelona	401 (£236 million)

But the milch cow may be running drier in the next 30 years. Alex Gillardi of NBC warns that the money may not last, at least not at these levels. Gillardi has been involved with three Olympiads over 11 years with NBC, and he has planned the bids for two summer Games. Apart from the rights fee for the Seoul Games, NBC spent a further $120 million (£67 million) on production. 'America has reached the peak,' he told us. 'There are no more "must have events".' Gillardi says the rights fees have gone too high, so that the networks can no longer rely on event coverage paying its own way.

Ross Greenberg of ESPN has much the same view: 'There is going to be a major bottoming out and falling out in the US in the mid-90s once the major TV contracts are up for renewal. There just can't be any more spending the way that there has been over the last four or five years.' Already, the IOC has reacted by arranging to have future winter and summer Olympic Games in different years.

Though the costs are astronomical the networks remain in sport for the ratings. Gillardi explained the 'game': 'If you don't bid for the Olympics you make more money for sure than if you do bid for the Olympics. But the Games are just before the start of the (new autumn) season. It should attract good ratings and thus catch audiences and advertisers for later programmes. It is something of a loss leader.'

CBS spent $1.1 billion (£616 million) in 1990 for a four-year exclusive contract with American baseball – 25 per cent more than the previous contract, shared by ABC and NBC. For baseball, this meant $10 million (£5.6 million) per team before a single ticket had been sold. Ellis Cashmore in *Making Sense of Sport* explains that 'in a business where a few rating points mean hundreds of millions of dollars in advertising revenue, CBS was prepared to absorb losses in the expectation that it could use the World Series to include October promotions for its prime time shows in its crucial autumn schedule, from which ratings are extrapolated. CBS effectively wanted to use the sport as an instrument for generating interest in its future programmes.' The question is, what will happen to this expensive contract next time?

Some commentators ask another question – is sport getting too big for its box? The big events have grown bigger and bigger in this TV age. Television is the magnet, the catalyst, the vital link in the chain. After all sport was not always a global language. In the early days the Olympic Games moved forward with faltering steps; Jules Rimet of FIFA fought an uphill battle to establish the soccer World Cup. Television has made the difference, turning minor into major. But this growth has turned into a grasping process; today there are more competitions and they occur more frequently. Some see a crisis of competence and values. After the US Superbowl in 1991, Jonathan Rendall said in the *Independent on Sunday*: 'From Mount Olympus to Tampa Stadium is a long journey ... the invention has taken over the inventor; a real-life Frankenstein indeed.'

Perhaps the change in market forces and prices signalled by Gillardi and Greenberg will halt the chain of invention. Sport generally will hardly be affected; the problems are only with the big events. On average, sport remains cheap programme material for TV. It is the second lowest cost per hour when compared to other programme areas like current affairs, drama or news. It continues to command good, often high, viewing figures.

Sport must stay in its own control room, making the decisions that are rightly its own. It must heed experts like Jack Nicklaus, who warned in 1984: 'Television controls the game of golf. It's a matter of the tail wagging the dog.' Sport must also look to its other friend and partner, the sponsor.

10 Cash registers

When it is a question of money, everybody is of the same religion
VOLTAIRE (1694–1778)

Wimbledon, 1990. A funny thing happened on the way to the final. An unseeded American, Zina Garrison, won match after match and reached the last two of the ladies' singles. Underdogs and non-seeds have often done well in sport. But this lady was Cinderella. She had nothing to wear to the Ball Game.

A hurried auction then took place. Miss Garrison was duly dressed in suitable gown and slippers to go to the Court. Of course, the Fairy Godmother was a well-known sponsor, an international supplier of sporting apparel.

The sight of sport and business together makes some people avert their gaze. There is the old traditionalist view that sport is not about money, but as we have seen that is now hard to believe, at least in most sports. For better or worse, sport and money are now married, or at least living together. Their union is often an uneasy one with the two partners striving to protect separate codes, interests and priorities.

The sports business encompasses a complex mix of activities and enterprises. There are empires of opportunity which sport has provided for the entrepreneurs of the world – both the honest and trustworthy and the decidedly shady. The list of sport's customers and partners is long – agents, coaches, managers and public relations consultants; equipment,

Come home to Marlboro country; there's no doubting the sponsor of this car at the Hungarian Grand Prix

169

clothing and machinery manufacturers; sponsors of every kind; commercial sport and health clubs; and a huge chunk of the media. The success of these businesses, and of sport generally, has also spawned a plethora of service industries which feed off sport and its participants, like corporate hospitality and specialist travel companies. All these are now part of the great, far-flung empire of 'sport'. Mixed together they produce a powerful cocktail of benefits, debates and disagreements. Not the least of the disagreements often come from friction caused by the largely voluntary and amateur managers of sport rubbing up against the professional, profit-oriented bosses of business. The most important benefit should be growth as more people are drawn into emulating their sporting heroes and heroines, because increased participation maintains and enhances sport's ability to deliver 'public good'.

Of course, there always was a sports business. Sports clubs and bodies have long let paying customers through the

Spot the spectator. Few get to see weekday county cricket even at the famous Lord's Cricket Ground in London

turnstiles. They still do, and still attract huge crowds, but for many sports, the gate income is no longer enough to meet today's ever rising costs. In English cricket, for example, weekday crowds are pitifully small. Robert McCrum observed in 1991, at the start of a match between Gloucestershire and Somerset: 'There's an air of anticipation among the 100 or so spectators scattered around the ground ... the uninitiated might be forgiven for thinking that the game was provided by the state for the entertainment of the homeless.'

Today's sports business is altogether broader based; it is streetwise, it is multi-national. It has grown fast, in the last 40 years in particular. Sport is now a vital and integral part of every developed economy in the world, as well as most of the less developed. In 1959 a survey by the Federal Reserve Bank of Philadelphia of 20 sports in the USA indicated that participants were spending over $8 billion (£2.85 million) a year directly on their sports with a further $10 billion (£3.56 million) indirectly on travel, facilities and connected activities.

In the UK, the sports industry is bigger than the agricultural, chemical and motor industries. A 1986 study by the Henley Centre for Forecasting in the UK on the 'economic impact of sport' in Britain suggested that direct annual spending on sport-related activities in the UK totalled £4.4 billion ($6.45 billion) – of which £770 million ($1.13 billion) went on shoes and clothing, £690 million ($1.01 billion) on sports goods, and £530 million ($780 million) on participation. The study found that sport accounted for 376 000 full-time paid jobs, as well as uncounted thousands of part-time and voluntary jobs.

Even those not interested in sport have felt the effects of this varied business on their lives. The technological revolution of the 1960s in the work place brought us more leisure time. To the standard working clothes and Sunday best wardrobes were added 'leisure' clothing – offshoots of the clothing developed for sportsmen and women – cleverly marketed by the manufacturers to make the wearer look and feel active, healthy and fit even if they never left their armchairs. Youngsters in particular have been the target of the sports fashion wear manufacturers. The advertising line is that they can look and act like their sporting heroes and heroines. All they (or their parents) have to do is buy the same (inevitably expensive) track-suit, shell-suit, sweat-shirt, T-shirt, trainers and so on. The result? In the midst of the general recession of 1990/91, one sports shoe manufacturer in Britain reported record profits of £8.2 million ($14.6 million) on a record turnover of £119.8 million ($214 million) – the equivalent of about 4 million pairs of trainers – against a turnover of £29.4 million ($52.5 million) in 1986. The company claimed to have 25 per cent of the UK market.

Nothing has promoted the sports business as much as television. The attraction for sponsors is sport's very public shop window – with TV this has become a huge, international shopping centre. Television reaches billions of people world-wide, providing a double-barrelled boost – to the sport and then to everything clinging to it. It is no surprise that millions of pounds, dollars and deutschmarks, etc., are invested in research and development and in the search for the latest high tech methods and materials.

The initial growth of the sports business was slow, although a few companies awakened early to the opportunities. As early as 1906, the Coca-Cola company was presenting ball and strike indicators, brightly emblazoned with the company's logo, to umpires at the baseball World Series. Henry Ford paid $100000 (£20000) for the rights to the American National Baseball League World Series in 1934. He had seen the sport's potential for promoting his vehicles; even in the years of the great depression, baseball continued to attract five-figure crowds. A health products company, Kruschen, sponsored the first British rugby league tour of Australia in the early 1930s. The first serious sponsorship in Britain didn't come until 1957, when the brewers, Whitbread, offered £6000 ($16800) in prize money to sponsor the gold cup race at Ascot. 'Sandown Park, and all supporters of chasing, have a great deal for which to thank Colonel Whitbread and his firm for the magnificent prize money they are offering for the Whitbread Gold Cup Chase ...' noted the *Sporting Life* on the day of the race. In the 1960s Gillette sponsored one-day cricket in Britain – and helped to launch a popular and profitable new form of the game. Initially, in 1963, the company paid only £6500 ($18 200) and sought nothing in return. In 1981 they withdrew, refusing to increase their fee beyond £130 000 ($263 000) – but also concerned with evidence that the public associated their name with cricket and not with their razor blades.

Motor racing too had some early sponsors. Oil and tyre companies provided much of the wherewithal for the cars to race, and erected a modest banner or two to prove it. Colin Chapman was the first, in 1968, to seek sponsorship support from *outside* the car industry. 'Profit isn't a dirty word anymore,' he used to say. 'Money is how we keep the score in motor racing nowadays.' Chapman's green Lotus took on the red and gold livery of John Player's Gold Leaf cigarettes. There were initial objections, but other manufacturers soon followed suit and the distinctive 'national' colours of past years were soon lost in history. Cars became flying cigarette packets, or a flashing kaleidoscope of different products and patterns. For a short period there were even condom cars.

However, in 1971, despite the spread of television, it is estimated that sponsorship of sport in the UK stood at a mere £2.5 million ($6.1 million). Commercial eyes did not blink for long; in ten years sports sponsorship multiplied out of all recognition. By 1982 it was worth £84.7 million ($148 million); in 1988 it stood at over £200 million ($356 million) with more than 2000 companies involved. In the same year, sponsorship in the USA is reckoned to have been about $1.5 billion (£843 million) with over 3500 companies involved. The spread is now worldwide; even in China the main provincial soccer teams carry company names. The Shanghai Snowflakes, for example, are named after a washing powder.

Like in any good business, growth was based on results. The Cornhill Insurance company were the first sponsors of

173

Test cricket in the UK, in 1977, at a cost of £1 million ($1.75 million) for 5 years. They are still the sponsors, at a rate now of £1 million a year. Both the company's objectives have been achieved. Spontaneous awareness of the company name has increased from 2 per cent to 16 per cent, helping to lift them according to Cornhill's Jeff Mayhew 'from the top end of the middle of the insurance company league into the first division. Thanks directly to this sponsorship, the only item in our promotional budget, we are now as well-known as the other major insurance companies.' Cricket has also served well in their second objective, to provide corporate hospitality for their network of insurance brokers. 'It's good value for money,' Mayhew told us.

The late 1970s and 1980s were a veritable gold-mine for some sports. The most attractive for the sponsors were obviously those sports which offered the widest television coverage – particularly athletics, football, golf, tennis and motor racing – although these were also the most expensive. Increasingly the companies entering the sponsorship arena had a clear policy strategy and a set of objectives for their expenditure. They knew which target market they wanted to reach; the value of the sponsorship compared to other forms of advertising and marketing; how much they were prepared to pay to secure sole sponsorship of events; and crucially, how to measure the results after each event or contract.

The Unipart group of companies manufacture automotive parts. Originally part of British Leyland, they are now an independent company manufacturing and marketing parts for British and foreign car makers. It's the dull end of the business; no sleek cars to sell, only a finely tuned carburettor seal or an exhaust pipe. But Unipart have spread their image through sponsorship, and most of its goes into sport. Patrick Fitz-Gibbon, who is the group's PR manager, told us: 'Sport is something which everyone can relate to; everyone has been involved in sport at some time or other.' Over the years Unipart have sponsored darts, football, powerboating, ballooning, polo, and Formulas One and Three motor racing, rallying and saloon car racing, as well as choirs and calendar girls. 'Each has a purpose,' says Fitz-Gibbon.

Gone are the days when the managing director liked golf and therefore sponsored it. Now, sport is even obliged to provide precisely the vehicle the sponsor is wanting. 'Polo brought us exactly the image we wanted at the time,' says Fitz-Gibbon. 'Darts, on the other hand, gave us the audience buying our product; motor and rallying gives us development opportunities for product, and football ties us immediately into the local community.' Oxford United are Unipart's local football club, and the two have been associated for ten years; 'It's a way of paying back the community. Large companies need to be seen to be working with the community in which they live, and football can do it for us.' Like all the best deals, it suits both sides.

A lot of sports at a variety of levels would have disappeared altogether without sponsorship. Motor sport, which soaks up as much as any other sport, certainly couldn't exist without it. 'Eighty per cent of Tyrrell Racing's costs are covered by sponsorship,' Bob Tyrrell, the managing director, told us. Some of the costs are picked up by Unipart, but the main provider is Braun, the electrical company. Electric razors are not very sexy and as a rule young men don't use them. Braun wanted something tied with technology – that's where they made their reputation – and something that had charisma. What better than motor racing, with its exciting and fast-moving lifestyle image, as the perfect vehicle for their shavers and other products? The sleek black cars with the small white legend 'Braun' were soon known as 'Braun Tyrrells'.

The Grand Prix priority now is attracting and keeping sponsors as costs continue to escalate. In 1970, two years after they started in Formula One, the Tyrrell budget was £80 000 ($192 000); today it is nearer £20 million ($35 million). Bob Tyrrell ruefully discussed with us what he calls the 'downward spiral'. 'If you don't get results, you can't get or even keep your sponsors. If you don't get the sponsorship, you can't invest. If you don't invest, you can't compete.'

175

Sponsors want a full service, and results, but the sport itself has become a massive public draw. Grand Prix racing is beamed to an average of 96 countries and attracts on average 263 million television spectators per race, a total of 4.2 billion viewers each year. (Ten years ago, the total figure was a mere 900 million.) Only the Olympic Games and the soccer World Cup attract larger viewing figures and they only happen every four years. Every year, the sixteen races in the Drivers' and Constructors' World Championships – the official name now for the Grand Prix circuit – top the TV charts, especially in Brazil, Italy and Britain. No wonder Goodyear's racing manager, Leo Mehl, says: 'Value for money? You bet. There is no other promotional area in which we can get such a bang for the buck.' No wonder Peter Dunn of the *Independent on Sunday* newspaper said it 'is less of a sport these days than a commercial break doing 150 mph'.

Sadly, sports' governing bodies were not well prepared to get the optimum deal and benefits for their charges. Most of the voluntary administrators were inexperienced in negotiating sponsorship contracts. In 1988 the *Official Year Book* of the Men's International Professional Tennis Council admitted that no one had anticipated the huge growth of the sport either at a recreational level or as a professional game. 'Consequently the ITF (the International Tennis Federation), the players, the Grand Prix Committee and the Men's Professional Tennis Council when it was formed, were not equipped to deal with the problems presented by the commercialisation of the sport. As a result, tennis grew haphazardly and became almost unmanageable.'

Few sporting organisations had any forward plans or clear ideas about the way their sports might be developed (at grass roots or at élite levels) or the resources needed to achieve these plans. The result is that, despite considerable sponsorship receipts, even big TV sports such as athletics and tennis have failed to grow rich through sponsors. These sports – and also rugby union, soccer, cricket, golf, and hockey, for example – still require public subsidy each year in the UK.

176

Partly because they foresaw restrictions elsewhere, alcohol and particularly tobacco companies were in the vanguard of sports sponsorship. And sport's demand for cash overruled all other concerns. In the light of mounting evidence of the effects of smoking on health, tobacco's links with sport have long caused the most heated debate, especially in Europe. For the companies concerned, product-link with healthy and whole-some physical activity has obvious benefits. And sport provides them with one of the few remaining public advertising vehicles, as the advertising of cigarettes on television is banned in many countries around the world.

The television reporter and writer, Peter Taylor, argued in his book, *The Smoke Ring – Tobacco, Money and International Politics*, that tobacco sponsorship 'enables the companies to associate cigarettes with healthy, glamorous and life-enhancing activities ... and above all enables (the tobacco companies) to get round the ban on advertising cigarettes on television. Tobacco sponsorship is designed to change the public perception of cigarettes and the companies who deal with them.'

Peter Roebuck, Somerset cricketer and journalist, is fiercely critical of the sports bodies for allowing themselves, in his view, to be ensnared by the tobacco companies. Writing in the British *Sunday Times* in 1991 he said: 'Tobacco barons cannot be blamed for this involvement. Doubtless they can hardly believe their luck. They spend a small part of profits made from their killer drug in sport and everyone says they are terrific, loyal and generous. No, it is the sporting bodies who are to blame. Sport need not rely on tobacco money because other sponsors can be found.'

In the UK the sponsorship of sport by tobacco companies is governed by a continuing voluntary agreement between the Minister for Sport, and the Tobacco Advisory Council. As well as total spend (which does not have to be made public) the agreement restricts branding and signage at televised events; the type of promotional material produced for spon-sored events; press, poster and cinema advertising; and com-

177

panies' use of particular brand names in event titles. It requires companies to 'exercise special care to ensure that (their sponsorship) does not attach to activities in which the majority of participants is under 18 years of age, or to events designed to appeal to audiences predominantly under 18 years of age'. David Teasdale was the senior civil servant responsible for the last set of negotiations on this agreement on behalf of the Minister for Sport. He recalls it as a 'classic Whitehall compromise'. 'It serves to prevent the further exploitation of sport and its media opportunities by the tobacco companies, without setting the clock back. It forestalls major rows with the various sports, which want to keep the money, and with the tobacco companies, which want to keep investing.' Seb Coe, who was involved in the debate as a Board member of both the Sports Council and the Health Education Council, has always counted himself with those who are against any publicity for smoking and against any tobacco links with sport, and to them the agreement looks a very bad compromise indeed: 'I've always argued that sport should not, at any price, let itself be linked directly with unhealthy activity and smoking has to be a prime example.'

Why does sport not take a tougher line? Many sports bodies have been linked with tobacco companies for a long time and found them to be good sponsors. Some are sympathetic to the smoking cause. Some share the view expressd by Peter Cooper, Chief Executive of the RAC Motor Sports Association who does not believe that 'anybody will start smoking simply because a tobacco manufacturer has sponsored a race or rally'. The General Secretary of the Central Council of Physical Recreation, Peter Lawson, takes a broader line: 'If the British government wants to move people off smoking then they should make it illegal. The government gets £20 million ($35 million) a day in revenue from tobacco – thus, sport gets three quarters of one day's public revenue on top, about £15 million a year (his estimate). And sport is struggling for support; without sponsorship, sport would wither.'

Other sponsors could no doubt be found, although in the

178

buyers' market that would inevitably follow the wholesale cessation of tobacco sponsorship, prices might go down. But the problem remains that by continuing to accept tobacco sponsorship, whilst espousing the inherent 'good' and wholesomeness of sport for youngsters in particular, sport lays itself open to criticisms of hypocrisy. Perhaps it has to decide finally where its priorities lie – in business, or in providing 'public good'. The last word might to go Steve Davis who said on winning the Embassy World Snooker Championship in 1981: 'I'd like to thank Embassy, but unfortunately I don't smoke.'

It was only a matter of time before sponsorship was attached not just to the sport but to its individual stars as well. Today top players and athletes can earn far more from promotions and product endorsements than they do from playing their game. In a world of big numbers, sponsorship for the top stars attracts big money. The British *Independent* newspaper dubbed tennis ace Ivan Lendl the 'six million dollar man' and said that Lendl was dressed to make a killing every time he stepped out on court. 'From head to foot, from sunglasses to tennis shoes, the world champion is estimated to be worth $6 million (£3.7 million) in endorsements by various companies – three times his winnings last year (1987). Some $2.5 million of that figure is derived from exhibitions and public appearances. Game set and cash to Lendl.'

Annual payments of £100 000 ($179 000) for product endorsements are now commonplace, and for good reason. Sports stars sell products, in staggering numbers. According to Neil Wilson, in *The Sports Business: the Men and the Money*, sales of Puma tennis rackets increased from 15 000 to 70 000 after they had signed up Boris Becker in 1975. Sales shot up to an amazing 300 000 in 1986. 'The company believes that Becker's Wimbledon victories generated sales of $50 million (£34 million),' notes Wilson.

Many top players endorse the equipment of their particular sport. In 1991, Nick Faldo was the world's number one golfer; he had a contract with Mizumo golf clubs said to be worth

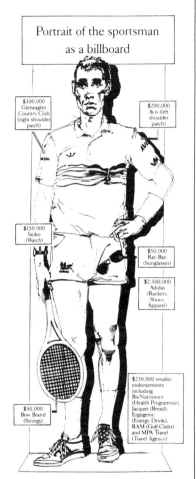

Portrait of the sportsman as a billboard

$300,000 Gleneagles Country Club (right shoulder patch)

$200,000 Avis (left shoulder patch)

$150,000 Seiko (Watch)

$50,000 Rav-Ban (Sunglasses)

$2,500,000 Adidas (Rackets, Shoes, Apparel)

$250,000 smaller endorsements including BioNutrionics (Health Programme), Jacquet (Bread), Ergogenic (Energy Drink), RAM (Golf Clubs) and MPA Travel (Travel Agency)

$50,000 Bow Brand (Strings)

The six million dollar man, or the sportsman as a billboard. In 1988 Ivan Lendl was the world's No. 1 tennis player, and was estimated to be worth about $6 million in endorsements, appearances and exhibitions – some three times the total of his tennis winnings

£7.5 million over 5 years. He also had one with Pringle sweaters estimated as worth approximately £10 million ($17.9 million) over 10 years.

Reebok have become a major manufacturing and marketing force in recent years. Started in 1895 as a small Lancastershire based shoe manufacturer, Reebok has grown into a multi-million dollar supplier of sportswear to the world (sales figures of $688.3 million (£385 million) in 1990). Reebok now sponsor more athletes in the UK than any other company, and not surprisingly have a very clear view about what they want from it. 'We don't look for the superstars, like Nike and Adidas do,' one of the brand managers, Tony Linford, told us. 'We prefer to sponsor many more people from junior level, who will then spread the Reebok word.' Sometimes the targeting of junior players brings an unexpected bonanza. From 1987 they helped an unknown young German tennis player named Michael Stitch; at Wimbledon in 1991 he suddenly became very well known when he won the men's singles and he's unlikely to be forgotten for some time to come.

How do companies make these judgments? Seb Coe can see both sides as a 'poacher turned gamekeeper'. He was sponsored for running wear and shoes by the Italian company Diadora, and ended up as their UK licensee in 1988. In this capacity, he has a number of British footballers, like John Barnes and Tony Cascarino, under contract to wear and advertise Diadora football boots, and the company also sponsors what is now the Diadora Football League, one of the major semi-professional leagues in Britain, with nearly 90 clubs. 'The bottom line is that the endorsement has to help you sell more units of product,' says Coe, the businessman. 'But you also use this to help create an image in the market, or to establish brand identification and loyalty.'

In 1990, Diadora scouts learned about a diminutive young tennis player in Florida. Just 13 years old, she had not yet played a professional match, but Diadora signed her to a 4-year endorsement contract which could make her a dollar millionaire. Jennifer Capriati has already shown her potential,

180

both as a player and just as importantly, as a personality. But why should Diadora take such a risk with an untried player? Coe explains: 'America is a massive market for tennis products and important to any sportswear company. Capriati is from Florida, one of the big tennis playing areas, with an all year round environment; she's a nice, fresh faced kid with a strong family background – and half Italian.' But of course it takes much more than winning matches for a sporting star to be a winning investment. Like Capriati for Diadora, the star has to project the right image for the company, the product and the market.

Salomon, one of the top ski equipment manufacturers, have very fixed views about their preferred person package. Chris Hanna, the company's sales director for North America, describes the ideal combination as 'a winner who can speak well, especially if they can speak a few languages ... somebody who can present themselves well, (and) can speak well of the product.'

Sport has also learned the lesson of Hollywood, that some-

Climbing to the top of the endorsement market. The French climber Catherine Destivelle shows why she is successful at her sport and in attracting sponsors

times sex appeal is just as important as ability. The French climber Catherine Destivelle has about 20 endorsement contracts in an activity not usually successful in attracting such commercial interest. In tennis, Gabriela Sabatini is a hotter property than, for example, Martina Navratilova, although she has rarely been able to defeat her on court. Male performers also cash in on this: 'People ask for anything with Andre Agassi's name on it,' said Dick Dillon, UK sales director of Donnay the racket makers.

One of the biggest stars in recent times in Britain is the soccer player Paul Gascoigne, whose fame soared after the 1990 World Cup in Italy and not simply because of his exciting skills. He struck an emotional chord in the massive worldwide TV audience for shedding tears on the pitch when it looked as if a yellow card from the referee might rule him out of the World Cup final. Now 'Gazza' endorses a wide range of products, many outside football – board games, deodorants, jewellery, calendars, school lunch boxes, to name a few. He has made a successful pop record and also has the largest fee for endorsing football boots of any other footballer (an estimated £100 000 plus ($179 000) a year). Says John Smith, who looks after sponsorship for the England team: 'There are some people who are born to be stars. The man has charisma. People can't take their eyes off him.' Gascoigne's business managers are Len Lazarus and Mel Stein: 'He has pop star status.' His earnings are many times those of earlier legendary soccer stars, even George Best, who had a similar charismatic appeal. 'But then,' says Lazarus, 'George Best didn't have Len Lazurus and Mel Stein.'

In this new world, players and athletes have increasingly needed commercial help and advice; someone to deal with the business and public relations aspects of their careers and leave them to concentrate on training and performance. Lazarus and Stein and the agents and managers like them, can make fortunes for themselves and their charges.

The agents' business in Britain probably started with a famous and popular sportsman called Denis Compton. He

He came, he cried, but he failed to conquer – England's Paul Gascoigne during the 1990 soccer World Cup Semi-Final against West Germany

was a dashing, cavalier figure and a great player of both cricket and soccer. In the spring of 1947 he returned to England from a cricket tour of Australia and was chatting at the docks with a journalist, Reg Hayter, as he packed luggage into the car he had left there some months previously. Inside the boot of the car were piles of letters he had been unable to deal with before he went away. Hayter offered to look through them and took the pile away. Many were commercial offers, of various kinds, usually to attend and speak at dinners and so on. Hayter realised that Compton needed some help with such correspondence and recommended another journalist called Baganal Harvey. Harvey became the first agent in the UK, soon arranging for Compton the first ever endorsement of a product by a sportsman. The product was Brylcreem and Compton's face and slicked down hair became one of the

Denis Compton, one of the great sportsmen in Britain after the Second World War, and the first to feature in an advertisement

best-known pictures in Britain, used in magazines and on billboards all over the country.

Jon Holmes is one of today's leading agents in the UK, looking after soccer players like Gary Lineker, John Barnes and Peter Shilton, cricketer David Gower and the England rugby captain Will Carling. 'I'm after the long term,' he says, 'which is not necessarily what the media want. I want people who can achieve in their sport what they dream about, and to use that to give them a base of something for the remainder of their lives.' He cites a great example in the American golfer, Arnold Palmer: 'Long before he reached a point where he could not win at golf, his other interests fulfilled him.' Not surprisingly, Holmes is an admirer of Mark McCormack and it was McCormack's 1967 book on Palmer that inspired him to try the agency business himself.

Mark McCormack started what is now the multi-national IMG (International Marketing Group) in an almost casual way. A lawyer by profession, McCormack was an accomplished amateur golfer. Playing one day with Arnold Palmer in 1958, Palmer asked for some friendly advice about a contract. Palmer was already finding it difficult to cope, personally, with the many and varied business demands on his time. McCormack was soon his full-time agent and manager. Now, IMG has an income of over $700 million (£400 million) a year with 43 offices in 20 countries, acting for sports stars and sports bodies all over the world, selling television rights, negotiating contracts and organising events.

Gary Player joined IMG in 1960, and Jack Nicklaus in 1961, giving McCormack, for the next ten years, control over the affairs of the world's three best golfers. Palmer remained the most lucrative for IMG, with off-course earnings estimated at $10 million or more. IMG now have over 75 of the world's top golfers and about 50 of the world's top tennis players under contract. Among the sporting bodies or events that IMG control or represent are the Wimbledon tennis championships, the US Masters and the Suntory World Matchplay golf championships. IMG also have interests in skiing, motor racing, ice hockey and has recently extended its interests to music, particularly opera.

Many within sport have questioned whether such wide-spread influence by one company is good for sport or for the players and athletes within it, and whether it is right for one company to be negotiating both the sponsorship of events and of the individuals playing in them. In the Suntory World Matchplay for example, in which the prize money exceeds £250 000 ($438 000), it appears difficult for any golfer other than those on IMG's books to gain entry. In 1988/89 Paul Azinger won the American Open golf championship, which should have assured his presence at most major tournaments, but he was not invited to take part in the World Matchplay event. He was not on McCormack's books. Neither was Jose-Maria Olazabal, rated the world's number two, who was not invited to the same event in 1991. 'They should call it the International Management Group Invitation,' said Olazabal, 'not the World Matchplay Championship.' Olazabal also told Britain's *Guardian* newspaper that he had rejected several offers to join IMG's golfing stable. 'I am very happy with my manager,' he said.

Concerns about agents like IMG and their role in sport were officially and publicly voiced in Britain in the 1983 report of the Committee of Enquiry into Sports Sponsorship, chaired by the former Labour Minister for Sport, Dennis Howell. Howell concluded that it was 'most undesirable that an organisation should be able to represent a governing body, sponsors, a significant number of top players, negotiate television, cable and satellite contracts, and sell merchandising rights. The situation is pregnant with conflict of interests and cannot carry public confidence.' The enquiry recommended that the government should refer IMG's relationship with various sporting events to the Office of Fair Trading 'to establish whether any monopoly situation exists', but no such examination was ever carried out. McCormack himself says: 'If you took 100 of those stories about our being ruthless or sharklike, 90 of them would centre on attitudes we have taken

185

on behalf of our clients. I think being ruthless, in the context in which it is applied to me, is really sort of a compliment.'

In the United States, the ruling bodies of professional tennis took IMG and other agents to court in 1985 because they thought they had too much power. Philippe Chatrier, who was the President of the International Tennis Federation, and the now defunct Men's Tennis Council, said that the agents were 'a cancer within'. The joint ITF/MTC lawsuit, filed in the US Federal District Court of New York, alleged that the agents were holding the game to ransom and operating a web of 'intimidation, fraud, and corruption'. The case was eventually settled outside the court so the allegations against agents were therefore never debated or judged. Chatrier told us: 'I still maintain it's very unfair to have agents owning tournaments and it's easy for them to persuade the players (to play).' He remains convinced that 'money is the biggest problem we face in tennis' and that there is too much of it around. When he retired from the presidency of the ITF in 1991, after fourteen years, he said: 'Our game is really in danger of dying from too much money. You cannot blame a brilliant young player who takes, say £120 000 ($210 000), which he or she is offered to play for just one night. But it gives them a totally false impression of life and what their tennis priorities ought to be.'

Chatrier's comments were echoed recently by Boris Becker, himself one of the richest stars in sport: 'Tennis is going in the wrong direction,' he told *The Times*, 'and one day it is going to fall apart completely. The money is so great now that it has to stop and I would not be disappointed if it did.'

Wimbledon's total prize money has risen from £26 150 ($63 000) in 1968 to over £4 million ($7 million) in 1991. But the money isn't all coming from the gate any longer, at least not directly; some comes from a new source of income – corporate hospitality.

At major sports events, the marquee is now an accepted part of the scenery. For example, Hertz rent a marquee at Wimbledon to entertain their clients – they give them food and drink and a ticket for the event. Naomi Graham has organised Hertz marquees at Wimbledon and other events for some years. At Wimbledon, they expect to have about 500 guests in the fortnight; their marquee can seat comfortably about 40 to 45 each day. 'Every one of our customers without exception are truly grateful to be invited to an event like Wimbledon,' she says. So Hertz invest for customer satisfaction, to 'offer thanks for the business we've received from them'. As one of Hertz's clients put it: 'We support Hertz, they entertain us, and it's a two way street.'

Wimbledon's chief executive, Chris Gorringe, says that corporate hospitality is; 'desirable, but not essential. We have to balance it with our prime service to the tennis fans and clubs.' Wimbledon first had marquees for corporate clients in 1975 and now has 46 used by about 110 different companies. There is 'a healthy waiting list', but Gorringe believes the service is about at its limit, which is governed by the number of seats available. In 1991, just under 10 per cent of Centre Court tickets went to this sort of customer and Gorringe believes it would be difficult for his All-England Club Committee to allow a higher proportion, without upsetting the essential balance.

In any examination of the sports business, 'balance' is an oft recurring word. Sport is at the centre of a spider's web of differing business interests. Those interests may conflict, as we have seen. Boxing, a conflict sport in another sense, gives a number of examples. Boxing managers are frequently also the promoters of their fights. Barry McGuigan, WBA (World Boxing Association) world featherweight champion in the mid 1980s, subsequently had serious disputes with his manager. In 1990 he said: 'a manager's job is to go out to get the best deal possible for his boxer; the promoter is out for the best deal he can get for himself, keeping the boxer's wages low. A system which allows an individual to be both manager and promoter is wrong; it is the nearest thing to a slave's contract.'

Don King personifies the power and control that a boxing

American boxing promoter Don King, the face that launched a thousand fights

promoter can gain over both his clients and the sport itself. King, the 'black Samson', as he calls himself, has promoted 225 world title fights since being released from the Marion Correctional Institute in Ohio in 1971, after serving less than four years for first-degree manslaughter. Some of the keys to King's success have been his close ties with big names like Muhammad Ali and Mike Tyson. He was also one of the first promoters to organise television deals with pay-per-view cable television. Another of King's close alliances, with Seth Abraham, senior vice-president for sports programming at HBO (Home Box Office), has enabled him to offer fighters more than other promoters. King himself describes his work, thus: 'I put together attractions, then exploit them. First you sign up the attraction, then you make a site deal to host the attraction. You sell it to pay-per-view and closed circuit … then you go out and promote the event like it's the second coming … That's what I do …'

Pyjama cricket! The Australian TV magnate Kerry Packer began a cricket revolution in the late 1970s when he bought up a clutch of the world's best cricketers for a televised world series. The games were played at night under floodlights, and traditional whites were replaced by fluorescent yellows, blues and browns for the opposing teams

Most sporting bodies cannot match King's flair, single-mindedness, or his methods. They have a more difficult balance to strike. On the one hand, they are responsible for the development of their sport, for spreading and 'growing' it as well as possible, while retaining its birthright of free and fair competition. On the other hand, they must maximise income from the new sources available from the world of business. The two hands do not always fit together. In the sports with the biggest public demand – like golf, tennis, soccer, American football, baseball and track and field – those two hands can become separate fists. High quality administration is needed – with modern, professional skills. Not all sports bodies and clubs have it. We must also remember, however, that sport is, as Peter Lawson, observes: 'a business with a difference. The board of management usually do it for nothing, and any surplus is reinvested in the sport.' This has not been recognised by all sporting interests, and a major conflict remains unsolved.

The two languages, of sport and business, have not always merged. At the local level, sport remains the corner shop, run by the family. When it gets bigger, it becomes a self-help co-operative, staffed by volunteers. The American folk singer Bob Dylan, a genius for the *bon mot*, said: 'Money doesn't talk, it swears.' The language of sport can also be strong. Over the next decades, if sport and business have regard for each other's feelings, they won't need to employ interpreters – or separate agents.

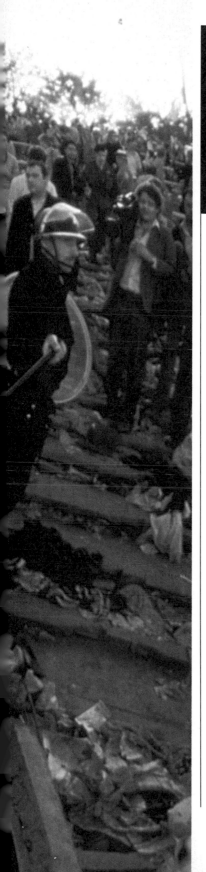

11 The violent tendency

Violence suits those who have nothing to lose
JEAN-PAUL SARTRE (1905–80)

They were nearly always anonymous, but unlike most urban terrorists, they never bothered to hide their faces. They liked the cameras; they enjoyed their notoriety. One such English soccer fan said: 'You go to other people's grounds, you run 'em, it's just enjoyment all the time ... Like a tennis player gets all geared up for play, we get geared up to fight ... Tribal, innit? Football is one tribe against another. We fight 'cos we like fighting.'

Such men brought the word 'hooligan' into the newsrooms of Europe in the 1980s. Unfortunately for the Irish, it was originally the name of an Irish family in south east London notorious for what the *Oxford Dictionary* calls 'ruffianism'. 'Hooligan' became attached to any street rowdy or trouble-maker. It later became attached to sport through one game in particular, soccer, and through one country especially, England.

Spectators of any sports may break boundaries and rules. Crowds invading the pitch after a great match, or a home victory, are a standard expression of collective triumph and pleasure. But in soccer hard men have used its venues and

During the Liverpool v Juventus European Cup Final in Brussels in 1985 39 people died on the terraces, and over 250 were injured. It was almost the death of what the Italians call 'the beautiful game'. English clubs were banned from European football for the next six years

191

events as vehicles for their aggressive, threatening, disorderly and on occasion murderous behaviour.

At its ugliest extreme, bad behaviour by spectators at sporting events has led to thousands of serious injuries and hundreds of deaths. We have already described how a soccer game and its spectators provided the spark which lit the tinder-box of war between Honduras and El Salvador. In recent years, spectator violence has very nearly caused the death of soccer.

In the last 30 years, crowd trouble at soccer matches has become part of the sporting life, with headline stories of fights, skirmishes, and even riots – between rival supporters, who have been dubbed 'savages', 'mindless lunatics', 'animals', and more besides. Many called this the 'English disease', exported, like sport itself in Victorian times, to the four corners of the world. But spectator violence at sporting events has in fact had a long history. Crowd fights were a regular feature of Roman gladiatorial games. In Constantinople, in Turkey, the wooden stadium was burned down no less than four times by unruly mobs between 490AD and 532AD. Rival fans of different chariot teams actually joined together, in 532AD, to protest against unpopular government officials. Promises by the Emperor Justinian to replace the officials fell on deaf ears; fighting broke out, the army was called in, and an estimated 30 000 people lost their lives.

In her book, *Cromwell Our Chief of Men*, Antonia Fraser reports that in the English Midlands in 1655, it was considered necessary to ban football matches and race meetings in order to preserve the peace. Later in the seventeenth century, more matches and race meetings had to be banned because of incidents of public disorder. In 1890 at a football match in England between Burnley and Blackburn the referee was attacked by stone-throwing crowds of supporters. In 1909 at Hampden Park football ground in Glasgow, over 6000 spectators vandalised the pitch and buildings and fought with policemen; 54 policemen were injured along with 60 spectators.

More than a game; a product. (*Top left*) Stefano Modena, top driver for Tyrrell Racing (*Pascal Rondeau/Allsport*). (*Top right*) John Lowe, world darts champion, 1987 (*Unipart*). (*Bottom left*) The yacht *New Zealand* in the America's Cup, 1986 (*Allsport*). (*Bottom right*) Nick Faldo, British winner of the US Masters and Open Championships (*David Cannon/Allsport*)

(*Overleaf*) Flames engulf the old stand at Bradford City football ground in the north of England, killing more than 50 people, 11 May, 1985 (*Syndication International*)

Frenzy for a loose ball: the San Francisco 49ers and the Denver Broncos at the 1990 Superbowl (*Rick Stewart/Allsport*)

King penguins on ice: the Los Angeles Kings play the Pittsburgh Penguins (*Robert Beck/Allsport*)

(*Overleaf*) Hot air rising! (*Allsport*)

Moths to a flame: the opening ceremony for the Seoul Olympic Games, 1988

(*Pascal Rondeau/Allsport*)

Violence has flared in other countries of course. A survey in America uncovered 312 cases of violence and disturbances across 13 different sports between 1962 and 1972 – ranging from 97 at baseball games, to 10 at motor car and motor cycle races, and two at air sports events. In one incident in 1955 there was riot after an ice hockey match between the Detroit Red Wings and Montreal Canadians. The fighting inside the stadium spread outside; shops over 15 blocks were looted, other buildings and cars were damaged and set on fire.

But worldwide, soccer heads the spectator violence league table, by a large margin. The list of major clashes is a sorry litany of viciousness and bad temper. In 1964, at a match in Lima, Peru, 318 people were killed in a riot and more than 500 were injured. In 1968, 74 people were killed at a match in Argentina. In 1982, 69 were killed at a match in Moscow, and 29 died at a game in Colombia. Throughout the 1980s regular incidents of spectator violence at soccer matches, resulting in serious injuries and sometimes death, occurred in particular in Italy, Yugoslavia, Turkey, China, Russia, Holland, Belgium, Germany, Greece, France and England.

A scene from Basle in Switzerland, Juventus v Porto. Rioting fans were regulars around Europe during the 1980s

Such events turned everyone into horrified spectators. The urgent question tortured supporters, administrators and players alike – why did this happen to soccer? Why has soccer provided the rock on which the 'hooligan' limpets seemed to find such an apparently ideal home, with such dire consequences?

The questions launched a plethora of research studies, public enquiries, and reports by academic institutions, sociologists, criminologists, psychologists, sports organisations, and governments. In England there is even a centre for research into spectator violence at Leicester University, funded by the football pools companies. Answers and solutions have proved elusive. A few common threads have been identified. The majority of individuals who display aggressive, threatening, abusive and violent behaviour at sporting events (and indeed elsewhere) are male, working-class, and in their teens or twenties. In the 1960s they might have joined protest movements; earlier this century they might have been called to war. In earlier times still in the heart of the Amazon basin, in parts of Africa or in the rain forests of Borneo, they would be entering 'manhood', and proving it through participation in traditional, initiation, religious and hunting rituals.

Most incidents occur when these young males are in groups or crowds; and where both the good and bad emotions triggered by sporting events are heightened, sometimes to fever pitch. 'Territory' seems to be another important factor. These 'fans' will protect and defend their particular end or part of a stadium against others who seek to encroach upon, damage or criticise it. They will defend their 'tribe'.

Many other sports are blessed with as fervent support as soccer and some have suffered, on occasion, bouts of crowd misbehaviour. But none has suffered from such prolonged and vicious violence.

Sir Norman Chester, an Oxford University don, loved football and made various studies of the game he called 'the spectator sport of the masses'. He noted in 1984 that Britain's other major team sports, like rugby and cricket, 'on the whole

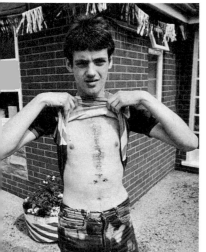

England supporter Mark Buckley was caught up in one of the violent incidents during the 1982 World Cup in Spain

draw upon a rather higher social stratum and in any case attract comparatively few spectators.' He believed that other social factors were at work: 'League football is the only sport which attracts large numbers to travel to away games. This is a comparatively recent phenomenon, made possible by the five-day working week and the greater ease of travel ... The significance of this social change is that a great deal of hooliganism occurs in confrontations between home and visiting supporters.'

Sir Norman encouraged the work of the Leicester University team in their research into football, and the facility at the university now bears his name. The Sir Norman Chester Centre has identified a number of factors that have influenced crowd behaviour. These include changes '... in the "rough" and "respectable" sections of the working class, and in relationships between them; changes in the mass media, above all the emergence of TV and the tabloid press ... and the recent virtual collapse of the youth labour market.'

The co-director of the Sir Norman Chester Centre is John Williams, whose early experience with hooligans was a close one. As part of the Leicester University research project to study the problem he infiltrated gangs attached to particular clubs. He spent some months 'underground' in the early 1980s with a tough band who followed Leeds United, a club with a bad reputation. It was this first hand knowledge, some gained on the fields of battle, that earned the research team's reputation.

We asked John Williams why there had been an explosion of violence in the 1980s? 'Because the game had literally run down its batteries,' he said. 'Some people have suggested a link with other disasters in public places like Zeebrugge and King's Cross; society (had) become less concerned about the community, about each other ... The focus was on making things pay rather than saving things for public benefit.'

Whatever the causes, firm action was not immediately to hand. Instead, football's hands were being wrung – all too frequently. Clubs seemed all too ready to cram more and more spectators into the ground, and all too reluctant to spend money modernising their Victorian stadiums and provide better amenities and facilities. They came to argue that football hooliganism was society's problem, not theirs; that it was unfair to blame football for the growing number of violent incidents which occurred miles away from the stadiums, in city centres and railway stations. They waited for someone else to solve their problem. Most of all, they looked to politicians.

In 1975 the government introduced 'Safety at Sports Grounds' legislation after 66 people had died and 140 were injured at the Ibrox stadium in Glasgow in 1972. This tragedy was not the result of spectator misbehaviour or violence. The crowd had started to leave just before the end of the Rangers and Celtic match on New Year's Day. Suddenly there was the noise of a late goal, some turned back, and in the melee, people were crushed against steel barriers which eventually gave way. The resulting legislation forced the larger football clubs to make certain safety improvements at their grounds. Most pleaded poverty, despite the millions of pounds they had taken in gate receipts in the preceding decades (when over 16 million people each year had flocked to football). The public debate led to the setting up of the Football Grounds Improvement Trust, and later the Football Trust, funded by the football pools companies. Today the pools provide about £9 million ($16 million) annually which can be spent on ground improvements.

Abroad too, English soccer fans developed a violent reputation. By the early 1980s, there was hooliganism all over Europe, and it was a worrying problem particularly for football authorities in Germany, Holland, Belgium and France, as well as England. However, in the main, only English fans travelled with their teams in significant numbers. And only they caused real mayhem on foreign fields.

Despite careful precautions and heavy security, there were violent incidents at the World Cup in Spain in 1982. The following year, in Luxembourg, an international against England was followed by running battles and looting in the

England's exports – this time to Turin, Italy, in 1980. Only the English seemed to take their hooligans abroad with them

196

streets, lasting many hours. And it was the first time such scenes had been witnessed in the principality. The British Consul told the Minister of Sport, Neil MacFarlane, that 'this one night has undone years of hard work on behalf of Her Majesty's government.'

The government remained reluctant to grasp the nettle in soccer's garden. But in 1984 they set up a working group comprising representatives of the Departments of the Environment (which contained sport) and Transport, the Foreign and Commonwealth Office and the Home Office to 'examine all the possible options'. One of the authors of this book, David Teasdale, then a senior civil servant in the Department of the Environment, chaired the group. Its report in 1984, 'Football Spectator Violence', contained recommendations covering domestic and international games, directed at law enforcement agencies, the football authorities and government. The report noted that '... violence at domestic football matches is sporadic and local and associated with a relatively small number of clubs ... its prevention depends upon the effective application of measures locally.' But national co-ordination was necessary as were some more general measures.

The working group also noted the responsibility of the media to report 'in a balanced way' and said that 'reporting of football violence is often exaggerated and inaccurate.' Hooligans relished the cameras and the notoriety. The report concluded: 'We understand the concern to seek an absolute, even a draconian, solution to this problem, but we believe that none exists which is both reliable in its effect and fair in its impact.'

Sometimes, the pace of change in public policy is controlled carefully by governments. But sometimes change is dictated wholly by events – sudden, unplanned, unforeseen. Such was the fate and direction of the Thatcher government on football, the following year, in 1985.

In February, Luton Town played Millwall FC in the FA Cup on a Wednesday evening. There was a riot after the game; 'fans' pulled up seats, threw them, with other missiles, and charged police across the pitch. There was hand-to-hand fighting; millions watched, in horror and fascination, on TV. One viewer was Margaret Thatcher, the Prime Minister, and the following morning she announced that the government would no longer tolerate such events and called the football authorities to account, in urgent meetings at 10 Downing Street.

At last, sport was at the top table – but for entirely the wrong reasons. The Government was concerned with law enforcement, with people's safety, with the nation's reputation rather than the good of football. 'Putting the house in order' was the imperative of the moment. Immediate steps included transferring the England against Scotland match in May from London to Glasgow. Ted Croker, Secretary of the Football Association, complained that the move 'has been forced on us and is a very sad testimony to the state of the world we live in.' Dennis Howell MP, for the Labour opposition, described the move as 'surrendering ... running away and declaring no-go areas for football matches'.

During the government talks with the Football Association and the Football League one FA official decided that attack was the best means of defence. He voiced what people in football felt, keenly: 'What we want, Prime Minister, is for you to get your hooligans out of our game,' he said. Mrs Thatcher found football's representatives hard going. The two football bodies had a history steeped in suspicion rather than co-operation. Responsibility for decisions was not as clear cut as Thatcher liked. There was deadlock on the issue of membership cards, which she favoured and they did not. An impasse was reached.

Then, again, tragic and unforeseen events clouded the issue. On 11 May 1985, there was a monstrous fire in the 76-year-old main stand at Bradford City football ground in the north of England. Over 50 people lost their lives. Again, the TV pictures brought the tragedy instantly and unforgettably to national attention. The following morning David Teasdale

199

visited the site with the Sports Minister, Neil (now Sir Neil) MacFarlane. 'We were acutely conscious of walking through the ash of human remains,' Teasdale recalls, 'I felt you could still hear the cries of anguish, as people tried to get away from the flames. But the gates out at the top had been locked and were not opened fast enough. This was a tragedy of an old, neglected stadium, part of the financial problems of an old, neglected game.'

John Williams, from Leicester University, was at the match. He observed that 'the younger spectators were not very concerned about the welfare of the older ones.' He argues that generally the 80s were a decade 'when it was less fashionable to look after and help each other'. Bradford's chairman made no bones about the state of his club's stadium: 'I am ashamed of the ground and I am ashamed when people come to Bradford and look at the ground. In a nutshell, it is a shit pit.' Over the years, such clubs had not invested in their facilities. The FA chairman, Bert Millichip, said that following this tragedy: 'without the slightest doubt, there are going to be a number of clubs to whom the fire authorities will say "No supporters will be permitted on to your stands unless and until there are new safety precautions".'

Mrs Thatcher was dumbfounded, and for once without a solution: 'We just want to do everything possible to see it doesn't happen again.' British soccer was reeling. Bradford was no worse than many grounds up and down the country. Action and money were needed urgently for the safety of spectators in grounds as well as to repel and control hooligans.

To make matters worse, on that same Saturday, the last of the 1984/85 league season, the hooligans struck again at a match between Birmingham and Leeds. One boy was killed, and over a hundred people were injured. Newspaper headlines and pictures featured the 'Faces of hatred'. It was a black day for soccer. To assess matters the government appointed Mr Justice Popplewell to conduct an official inquiry into soccer violence and safety.

Tragically, within a few short days, while those events

200

settled into a shocked public mind, on 29 May the European Cup Final was played at the Heysel Stadium in Brussels. Liverpool of England played Juventus of Italy. Everyone thought we had now seen all there was to see in crowd and soccer trouble. But, again on TV, this time to a huge European audience, 39 people were killed and 250 or more injured as violence erupted between rival fans.

Once again, Mrs Thatcher had to face the cameras at 10 Downing Street. She said the: 'Liverpool fans have brought shame and disgrace to their country and to football.' The pace of the meetings inside No. 10 became even more intense, as did the debate around Britain and Europe. The Italian Prime Minister, Bettino Craxi, said Britain was 'a country submerged in disgrace by the criminal actions of violent and irresponsible groups.' His Minister for the Interior, Oscar Luigi Scafforo, described British fans as standing for 'violence at any cost and in any case.' The strong feelings were repeated in European countries less directly affected. West Germany's *Bild Zeitung* newspaper asked: 'My God, why are these vandals allowed to leave the island? Never again let these visitors into a stadium.' German TV stopped the transmission of the match out of the respect for the dead, but the game was still televised in most countries, including Britain and Italy. *L'Equipe*, France's sporting paper, echoed the views and fears of many sports people: 'If this is what football has become, let it die.'

In London a leader in *The Times* on 30 May reflected on the essentials of football and the trends which had brought the game to this point. 'Peripheral factors loyalties, money making, feelings of community identity, national and local pride – have turned a simple game into one of the most powerful, popular activities in the sporting world.' But those 'peripheral factors' had become 'over dominant' and the sport was 'now as good as dead'. 'Soccer,' the article thundered, 'has been swamped, as though by a foul poison, by a persistent strain of criminal violence that grew out of the game's peripheral problems, but has now utterly abandoned the host that gave it its original life.' And *The Times* ended thus: 'For the cures to its crisis, football has to look further than its own disciplines and rules. The game is no longer the thing. The game has gone.'

Very nearly, it had. Now it really was Orwell's 'war minus the shooting'. Downing Street responded; measures agreed and implemented in succeeding weeks brought sport and football on to a war footing. The outcome was tighter enforcement by police and stewards especially at 'problem matches'; co-ordination with government and others of planning and arrangements for matches; effective segregation of rival fans; the speedy introduction of closed circuit television at all league grounds; legislation to ban alcohol at grounds; and the encouragement of family enclosures.

But it had to be 'Fortress Europe' as well as Britain. The Thatcher government recognised the demand and need for action across Europe too. David Teasdale was already the chairman of a Council of Europe working group which had produced an advisory document on spectator violence in 1984. Work began to convert advice into legislation, and active co-operation from all European countries as well as UEFA led to the passing in record time (in August 1985) of the European Convention on Football Spectator Violence. Mr Justice Popplewell described this in his report as 'a blueprint for European football, which has lessons for our domestic game'.

All this activity and attention was hardly the publicity soccer, and sport, needed. Opinion polls in 1985 confirmed the obvious; that a high proportion of people no longer found football attractive. They feared crowd disorder and found measures taken inside grounds (including police searches, segregation, etc) unpleasant and off-putting. It had become commonplace for up to 5000 policemen to be deployed at 40 or so football grounds each Saturday (an average of 111 per game). Some matches could have perhaps 350 policemen on duty. Such a police presence provided reassurance, and protection, but it was hardly an advert for health and football. Perhaps most damning for football, though few remarked on it at the time, was Popplewell's wry comment, in his interim

202

report, that: 'at Halifax Town there are ten times as many police on a Saturday looking after 1500 spectators as there are on the same ground on a Sunday when speedway takes place with some three times as many spectators.'

The final Popplewell Report, published in 1986, noted that he had invited all 92 Football League clubs to assist his enquiry with their views and advice: 'I have rather sadly to record that over 50...did not even take the trouble to acknowledge receipt of my personal letter.' He also added this postscript: '... the problems of football will continue long after I have returned to the more familiar and less turbulent routine of my official duties.'

These were low days; sport had taken the front pages, for the wrong reasons. In the general debate people agreed that the boil had to be lanced. Some argued that excessive or repressive actions could serve only to fuel the violence. But most believed strong, tough action was required. Many doubted whether the government actually understood the game, and its traditions; and just as many doubted whether the clubs and football's authorities were doing enough. It appeared that both sides failed to consult the supporters themselves, the vast majority of whom were law abiding citizens who simply loved the game of soccer and wanted to continue watching and supporting it in peace. Out of these difficult days grew an organisation to represent those supporters that still exists today, the FSA (Football Supporters Association).

Football inevitably lost some of its sponsors. The managing director of Fads, a chain of DIY stores, announced: 'We are pulling out of football because Fads is an upright and clean company. That is something which can no longer be said about soccer. It is a sick sport. We would rather sponsor netball.'

The siege of soccer by the hooligans continued into the late 80s. Officials in the Minister for Sport's office dreaded big matches, especially the international games. These games required comprehensive planning, encompassing domestic and foreign police forces, embassies, Interpol, air lines, ferry companies and tour operators, and other governments. It was a game of catch, and the hooligans were increasingly battle hardened and professional. They would hire coaches as ordinary holidaymakers and plan roundabout journeys to avoid checks *en route*. On one occasion such a group was identified late in the day, and only because they had left a number of their 'calling cards' at a ferry port in England. Rapid police enquiries soon identified the group and their vehicle. Forces across France and Spain were alerted and officials in London plotted their progress through reports of continuing aggressive behaviour, across the continent. Their coach eventually crashed in Spain. Its occupants were arrested and deported; some then got drunk at the airport and missed the flight home, and then had the gall to seek financial help from the British Embassy!

The World Cup Finals were always an area of special concern. David Teasdale recalls Mexico in 1986 in particular, when three British teams (England, Scotland and Northern Ireland) had qualified for the final stages: 'The planning that time was a great success, there were no major incidents, but I always felt that a key factor might have been the soldiers with a machine gun at every street corner! We could never match that in Leeds, or Manchester.'

But there was yet one more major tragedy on football's horizon, the disaster at Hillsborough in Sheffield in 1989. Like Bradford, this was not caused by hooliganism. Hundreds of Liverpool FC fans, there to see the FA Cup semi-final against Nottingham Forest FC, were channelled into an already crowded section of the ground. The awful crush at the front caused 95 deaths. This led Mrs Thatcher to appoint another judicial inquiry, this time under Lord Justice Taylor. His Report in 1990 recommended in particular all-seater stadiums. Once again, the football authorities pleaded poverty.

In the space of four years, the great British sport of soccer had been subject to the close inspection of two leading representatives of the judiciary, government studies, Council of Europe scrutiny, and Downing Street's attention; only the

204

Church was left. Some felt that Britain's football industry was most in need of divine intervention! According to John Williams at Leicester University, the Taylor Report did however mark a significant change: 'It clearly stated that the game was worth saving, and in spite of the gloom, created a sense of optimism.'

And things did get better. The 1990 World Cup in Italy was relatively trouble free. In Britain in the 1989/90 and 1990/91 seasons there were no major incidents, and, following their five-year exile after Heysel, English clubs have played again, safely, in European competitions. Most clubs now have sections for families, some have special children's clubs and even crèches. Stadiums are being improved and some already meet tougher safety standards, but to British soccer's shame there is still a long way to go to match standards enjoyed by Europe and the rest of the world. Even Soweto in South Africa boasts a soccer stadium surpassing anything in Britain.

But it is too soon to say if all the bad days have passed for ever. Those directly involved have obviously grown up a little and perhaps no longer need to prove their manhood. Perhaps, too, their successors on the terraces no longer thrive on such aggressive behaviour, though that is a dangerous assertion. Maybe, the near death of the sport itself brought everyone to their senses. Maybe, the measures introduced by football and by government have had the required effect. Maybe, the tragedy at Hillsborough was the final straw which broke the back of hard-eyed hooliganism.

Maybe the game in Britain needed a good old-fashioned footballer again. Sporting personalities can reflect their times but some can lead by example and Gary Lineker, the England striker and captain, has done much for his sport in the last five years to show that the old values can prevail in new times. At the 1990 World Cup, England won the first ever fair play award and their performance 'was important in re-shaping the agenda' according to John Williams. In 1991 Lineker himself received a unique, personal fair play trophy from FIFA. Lineker's agent Jon Holmes believes 'he has done a

fantastic job for the marketing and image of the game, post Heysel. He's been the acceptable face of football.'

Why did it all happen? Was society to blame, or football? The choice is too simplistic. British politicians of the 1980s will take different views, as will soccer administrators. John Williams says: 'It was probably the most important decade in the history of the game. Lots of key issues came to the fore ... in a variety of disastrous ways.' Williams believes that law and order was over emphasised and 'reigned to the exclusion of other equally important considerations'. For the government of course law and order had to be the major concern. Mrs Thatcher and her ministers believed that any government's first duty was the protection of the people and, for a period, the hooligans were a serious threat on a Saturday afternoon.

Saturdays may now be quiet again. English soccer has turned to arguments about its future; about a Premier League, and about who is to run the game. We cannot do better than to borrow Mr Justice Popplewell's postscript to his interim report, to echo these words of Matthew Arnold:

'Peace, Peace is what I seek and public calm;
Endless extinction of unhappy hates.'

'You'll never walk alone', the Liverpool theme song (from the musical *Carousel*) is the poignant epitaph on the gates to the club's famous ground at Anfield. Mourners stand and study the tributes left to the Hillsborough dead

12 The Olympic flame

The modern Olympic Games symbolise the struggle between man's ideals and the reality within which he must live

RICHARD ESPY, AUTHOR OF *THE POLITICS OF THE OLYMPIC GAMES*

Let's picture a spring morning in 1886. The early sun lights but scarcely warms the spires and green fields of Rugby school, in the centre of England. Baron Pierre de Coubertin, a French aristocrat obsessive in his search for ways to redress the moral and physical decline in his country, which he believed responsible for their defeat by the Germans in 1870, is standing with Dr Arnold. (Arnold was the famous Headmaster of Rugby School through *Tom Brown's Schooldays*.) Today they are watching the boys practising sporting and physical skills. Not for the first time in his visit, the Baron is struck by the code of discipline imposed and learned through sporting endeavour.

James Coote in his *History of the Olympics* claims that de Coubertin was much taken with Dr Arnold and his philosophy and regime. The French visitor concluded from his travels and studies that the success of Victorian Britain could be ascribed to 'the character of its ruling class whose attitude to life was formed by an educational system in which the physical counted above the intellectual, and the moral above both'.

This was a period when Britain under Queen Victoria was for some the centre of civilisation, the hub of an empire on which 'the sun never set'. It was a sharply divided, class

The stage awaits; the new stadium erected in Barcelona for the Games of the XXV Olympiad. Today the Games are the world's biggest single sports event

209

society, but it exported a strong set of moral values. It also exported sport – with its own rules and values. And perhaps the greatest sporting export, based on those rules and values – and through the visit of de Coubertin – has proved to be the modern Olympic Games.

Through the growth and events of the modern Games we can trace many of the issues discussed in this book. Sport has become big business, none bigger than the Games; the greatest champions have sought out the arena of the Games; and politicians have become involved. Why have the Olympic Games become so important?

One answer lies in history, ancient and modern. According to Homer, there were games staged by Pelops, the god of fertility, as early as 1370 BC. Various contests are believed to have been held in antiquity, consisting usually of chariot racing, wrestling, boxing, running, archery and discus. Games were held at Olympia when Clymenos, a descendent of Hercules, erected an altar there to his ancestor and promoted games in his honour. Clymenos was deposed by Aethlios, the first king of Elis, from whose name comes the word 'athlete'.

An ancient Greek carving depicting scenes from a very early Olympic Games

We know from records that there were regular Olympic Games for an unbroken period of 1168 years. The last, in 393 AD (the 293rd Olympiad), followed a ban on pagan religious festivals imposed by the Emperor Theodisius.

A key feature of the early Games was the sacred truce. During the Games, no one was allowed to take up arms; legal disputes were suspended; and there were no death penalties. (The terrorists at the Munich Games in 1972 were perhaps unaware of the ancient rule they broke.) The Greeks practised sport, not for its own sake, but for physical perfection and military proficiency. Competitors trained under strict supervision for 10 months, before the event. What price amateurism, in ancient times? And amateurism is not the only value we falsely ascribed to those days. Only men of pure Greek descent were allowed to take part. A distorted echo of this tradition was found in Hitler's attitude to the inclusion of Jews in the German team at the Berlin Games of 1936, as well as Jews and blacks in visiting teams.

Before Theodisius' ban, the Games had grown to a five-day programme. On the first day, the opening ceremony featured a solemn oath by contestants and judges alike against cheating. On the second day, they staged the pentathlon (running, javelin, discus, wrestling and jumping) and horse-drawn chariot races. The third day was reserved for three special races – the Stade, a race of just over 600 feet (said to have been measured by Hercules as the distance he could walk while holding his breath – and origin of the word stadium); the Diaclos, two lengths of the stadium; and the Doliclos, 24 lengths. Then there came wrestling, boxing and pankration (a no holds barred mixture of the former two). On the final day was the prizegiving, the thanksgiving and a banquet.

The 23 Olympiads of the modern era have grown with and through massive developments in communications and the Olympic movement itself has now changed dramatically. Cynics might say that only the name links the first modern Games in Athens in 1896 and the television spectaculars of the last two decades. The Games of 1896 were a small, amateur

event; by 1988 in Seoul, the Olympics had opened its doors to the rich professionals of tennis and soccer and was attended by 159 countries. Indeed 100 years after the rebirth, some believe that the IOC's choice of Atlanta as the venue for the Centenary Games in 1996 was based primarily on considerations of corporate sponsorship and television time zones.

The key event in the rebirth of the Olympic movement was an international conference on physical education in Paris in 1889, which the French government asked Baron de Coubertin to organise. The Baron was a brilliant educator and scholar. His visit to England, perhaps especially to Rugby school, reinforced his belief in the importance of physical culture and its value in international dialogue and contact. He used the Paris conference and a subsequent lecture tour to Britain and the USA to publicise his proposals for a modern Olympic Games. His efforts were rewarded by the convening of the first international Olympic congress in 1894, attended by 79 delegates from 13 countries (with messages of support from a further 21). The Congress decided unanimously that the Games should be reborn with the first being held in Athens, Greece, in 1896.

The Greeks had enthusiasm but, initially, little else; their country was close to bankruptcy. At one stage, Hungary was touted as an alternative, but they declined the offer. All sections of Greek society were asked to contribute. The Greek Olympic bacon was eventually saved by the modern Games' first sponsor – a rich merchant, George Averoff, who put up a million drachmas to fund the restoration of the old Olympic Stadium in Athens which dated from 300 BC. What a tradition Averoff began – if unwittingly!

The Games which finally started on 25 March, 1896, after a gap of 1503 years, were a local sports day compared to the late twentieth-century version. A mere 12 countries took part. Of the 500 contestants, 60 per cent were from Greece. There were just 14 competitors from the USA and eight from Britain. By comparison, the Games across the Mediterranean 64 years later, in Rome, attracted a then record number of 84 countries and 6000 contestants. In Munich in 1972 there were some 9000 competitors and officials from over 120 countries.

In 1896 some entrants were merely tourists visiting Athens at the time. One British tennis player entered the tournament simply to secure a court and a game. A French sprinter wore kid gloves to run in because royalty were present. Robert Garrett won the discus title for the USA in a genuinely

American Robert Garrett practised the discus for only two weeks before catching the boat across the Atlantic and defeating three Greeks in the first modern Olympics in Athens in 1896, much to local chagrin

amateur, opportunistic fashion. Having decided to enter, he practised throwing a steel discus for just two weeks before sailing for Athens. What he lacked in technique he made up for in enthusiasm. On arrival he discovered the 2kg discus to be used in the competition was far lighter and much easier to flight than the one he had used for practice. He won the competition by defeating three Greeks. The Greek crowd was shattered at their country's loss in the event, and Garrett posed for 'the folks back home' in a classic outfit that his feat, if not his talent, deserved. At least, the Greeks had a victory in the first ever marathon, an event suggested by the French delegate, Michel Bréal, to commemorate the heroic feat of Pheideppides in 490 BC. (Pheideppides ran from Marathon to Athens, a distance of 25 miles, with news of the Greek victory over the Persians.) Local and national feeling about the need for a home victory was illustrated by the shower of gifts offered to any Greek winner – including, from that first sponsor, the offer of the hand of his daughter with a dowry of a million drachmas. Miss Averoff's reaction to her father's generosity is not recorded. In the event, the eventual winner, Spiridon Luis, was already married. But he did not go without, enjoying other 'prizes', including free shoe polishing for life! Thus, running for reward was established at the very outset of the modern Games. Although the Olympic torch was not yet a feature the first flickering flames of commercialism were soon to become an incandescent blaze.

The next Games were in Paris in 1900, thanks to de Coubertin's influence. He swayed a debate at the 1897 Congress in Le Havre on whether the Games should always be in Athens, a decision which has had a crucial impact on the growth of the modern Olympic movement. But de Coubertin was a prophet honoured abroad rather than in his own country, and when the time came, French interest was centred on the World's Fair and on the construction of the Eiffel tower. The organisation and promotion of the Games in France were so poor that de Coubertin resigned from the committee. Foreign entries found it hard on arrival in Paris to get any information

214

about the competitions, including dates, times or venues. Even the title 'Olympic Games' was removed, and the event was called *Concours Internationaux Exercises Physiques et du Sport*. The event dragged on for two months.

The outstanding winners in Paris in 1900 were two Americans, Alvin Kraenzlein, who beat all-comers in the 60 metres, 110 metres and 200 metres hurdles and the long jump; and Ray Ewry, who won the standing high and the standing long jump – the hop, step and jump. So it seemed appropriate that the next Games moved from Europe to the USA – a country destined to play a major role in the Games thereafter. But in St Louis in 1904 the Games were again subsidiary to a World's Fair. It must be some consolation to the ghost of de Coubertin and his colleagues that the new movement should so outstrip the World's Fairs within a few decades.

The only event of lasting note at the St Louis Games was the marathon. President Theodore Roosevelt almost presented the winner's medal to a hoaxer, Fred Lorz, who had hitched a lift on a lorry for nine miles of the course. He was acclaimed the victor, when just in time, the real winner, another American called Thomas Hicks, tottered into the stadium. Another lasting memory was the diet of the competitors. It was based on buffalo meat. The Europeans could not stomach this and it is recorded that they survived largely on milk and boiled potatoes.

In 1906 there were unofficial Games back in Athens, staged by Greeks now worried at the loss of 'their' Olympic movement. Twenty-two countries sent over 900 competitors. But the organisation was poor and the event was never repeated. The 1908 Games were scheduled for Rome, but the Italians withdrew and London filled the breach. The White City Stadium was built for the purpose, with a concrete cycling track, a running track and a 100-metres swimming pool. London's Games were heralded as the best international sports meeting yet mounted. They set a new standard which helped secure the development and acceptance of the new movement. Baron de Coubertin himself wrote in his *Mémoires Olympiques*:

215

'Many similar great spectacles have since then (1908) passed before these eyes. Memories of the London stadium have never disminished by comparison. The enormous enclosure, black with people, vibrant with enthusiasm, distilled a sensation of (Olympic) strength that, as far as I am concerned, has never been equalled or inspired by other crowds at home or abroad. The circumstances, in addition, pitted the youth of the two Anglo-Saxon (nations) against one another with particular virulence, and gave birth within the Olympic body to a kind of test of muscular strength between their champions.'

The great stadium rang to the cheers of excited crowds for over 60 years. But the cycling track and the swimming pool were closed, and eventually the athletics track became a dog racing venue. In 1986 the site was acquired by the BBC for a huge new office and studio complex. The first building of a number was recently opened – sadly it is an indifferent architectural monolith, as sterile as the stadium was grand.

That first White City crowd witnessed another momentous

Then, they really ran in lanes. Kerr of Canada wins the 200 metres at the new White City stadium in London, built for the 1908 Games. Some 70 years later the stadium was pulled down, and a BBC office block is now on the site

216

marathon. Pietri Dorando of Italy became the first Olympic star, and his sudden fame around the world alerted sports bodies to the importance and potential value of such international contests. Dorando led the race but was spent when he entered the stadium and initially went the wrong way round. Having been corrected, he had to be assisted over the line and was disqualified. A sympathetic Queen Alexandra presented him with a special gold cup.

After great success in London, the Games gathered an increasing momentum that since has only been interrupted by war, except for two further periods of doubt and hesitation. The first came after the Second World War; no country seemed willing to restart the competition and in the end it was London again which played host. In 1948 the White City stadium again rang to the cheers of an Olympic crowd, though this time sharing the honour with other London venues, like the newly-built Wembley Stadium. The second came 30 years

The first world sporting star did not even win! Pietri Dorando of Italy was first into the stadium in the 1908 Olympic marathon, but was helped over the line and had to be disqualified. Public sympathy was such that Queen Alexandra presented him with a special gold cup

217

later, when the Olympics seemed to have become too big and too costly and were out of reach of the municipal budgets on which each Games were meant to depend. The financial burden of staging the event had become enormous. Fewer countries were eager to put themselves forward as possible venues. The watershed was in Montreal, in the mid-70s. By then, the expectation was that an Olympic Games demanded a full and impressive range of newly-built facilities; it was a city's and a country's opportunity to show off. It was two weeks of 'conspicuous consumption', to borrow one of the economists' clichés of the period. But Montreal's Mayor Drapeau was an opportunist, in the view of Charles Palmer, ex-chairman of the BOA, who 'brought forward Montreal's future town planning by a quarter of a century'. He invested in city projects like roads, rail, an airport, as well as fine sports facilities. It is often said today that the ratepayers of Montreal are still paying for the 21st Olympiad. But Palmer says the Montreal Olympics 'made money, like their predecessors from 1964 onwards. But all the city projects were lumped on to the Games' balance sheet. It's the redevelopment of Montreal that is still being paid for.'

The view persisted that any city hosting the modern Games meant incurring a crippling financial burden. Only Teheran and Los Angeles bid for the 1984 Games, and pretty soon Teheran withdrew. Fortunately this Hobson's Choice proved a great one for the movement. Cometh the hour, cometh the man; and the man was Peter Ueberroth, who showed that through TV income and corporate sponsorship the Olympic Games could be very profitable.

Today that is the received wisdom, and the IOC is now courted by major cities wanting the opportunity of a profitable place on the Olympic rostrum. For the Games of 1992, the IOC chose Barcelona ahead of enthusiastic pleas from Belgrade, Birmingham, Brisbane, Amsterdam, Delhi and Paris. For the centenary of the first Modern Olympiad in 1996, the IOC have chosen Atlanta against stiff competiton from Athens (the favourite), Melbourne, Toronto, Belgrade and Manchester. Afterwards there were very sore feelings in Athens in particular; 'The Greek Olympic Committee has irrevocably decided,' a statement declared, 'not to participate in any events marking celebrations for the 100th anniversary of the revival of the modern Olympic Games.' This was the Committee's 'minimum expression of disapproval'.

The final choosing these days involves a jamboree that is a mini-Olympics itself, with salesmen from cities around the world as contestants. Some 80 IOC members, and their wives, plus a retinue of staff, assemble to hear the final presentations from the cities wanting to host the Games. Nagano's place in Olympic history, for example, was decided at the Birmingham IOC Congress in the summer of 1991, on which the IOC spent £1.2 million. The Japanese city will house the winter Games in the year 1998. To make the decision, the IOC took over Birmingham's most luxurious hotel for a week. The Queen attended the opening ceremony, which featured a ballet, a light show, and marching Grenadier Guards. The competing cities spent a fortune too. Nagano flew a children's violin group from Japan to entertain the delegates as they arrived. One of their competitors, Osterlund in Sweden, flew in a Swedish choir.

Outside the conference arena, where the presentations and the deliberations take place in secret, the atmosphere is strictly commercial. All the sponsors who have bought the right to use the five Olympic rings on their products for the relevant period have stalls. The movement which was virtually broke in 1972 is now living and thriving like no other.

The IOC does not make public exactly how its decisions are made, but we know that the 82 members all have a vote and the last city drops out after each round of voting until one city is left. The voting figures emerge only unofficially. Charles Palmer has served on various IOC commissions and committees (although he is not an IOC member). His former posts include the presidency of the International Judo Federation (1965–79), Secretary General of GAISF (General Association of International Sports Federation) (1975–85)

219

and chairmanship of the BOA (1985–88). We asked him how the IOC approached decisions on a host city. 'There is no standard attitude, or general reason for a decision,' he said. 'For some members the key point is what's best for the competitors. For others, the concern is to vote with their own bloc – the Latin Americans, for example. There have even been suggestions in the press that some members pledge their votes to the highest bidders – but no one has ever come up with any evidence to back up such claims.'

We must expect any loyal and committed Olympian like Charles Palmer to pick his words carefully, on such delicate matters. In fact, rumours are rife after IOC votes and there are many who claim to know the reasons why members plump for one particular choice and not another. For Peter Lawson, General Secretary of the Central Council of Physical Recreation in the UK, 'the process is nothing more than a lottery. The IOC selection process defies logic, and fortunes have been lost. It's a very costly game to play under the present rules.' What is surprising, according to Lawson, is that so many cities are prepared to take part. Some feel that the whole thing is a fix, and worse, a fix oiled by 'gifts' from cities to members. The Princess Royal, one of the two British IOC members, has criticised the giving and taking of gifts. No one denies that IOC members receive 'hospitality' from bidding cities. As this involves a first class air ticket, hotels and entertainment, it is not insignificant. Athens supporters complained in 1990 that 'Coca-cola has bought the Games for Atlanta.' After the 1991 Birmingham Congress, Salt Lake City were suspicious of the resources expended by Nagano.

But Alex Gillardi, from the American TV network NBC, who's been involved in three Olympic bids, dismisses the stories as 'sour grapes'. He cited one example: 'People complained after Barcelona's win that (the city) had paid for all the (IOC) delegates' telephone calls for a year. What happened was that delegates were simply given a cheap gift of a plastic telephone with the city's logo on it to take home. It cost just a few dollars!' Charles Palmer also doubts there is

220

any firm evidence about the value of other sorts of gift, 'or of any doubtful practice', and offers another slant on the issue. Palmer says he has considerable sympathy for IOC members from poorer countries, in Africa, and even Eastern Europe: 'For the African it is *de rigueur* to look after one's family and friends. They have no tradition of Western ethics about gifts, nor of old Victorian principles. They are expected to make the most of their situation. Similarly, I remember serving on committees with colleagues from the Eastern bloc, who simply had no foreign exchange. Their daily expenses would just cover a cup of coffee. Fortunately, now the IOC picks up everyone's daily expenses.'

As bigger and bigger sports events have been played out on the world's stage, the Olympics reigns supreme. Its attractions are now such that the movement might have been invented by the media barons in the late twentieth century, had it had not been created already by the imagination of de Coubertin at the end of the nineteenth century. The Games have progressed from the amateur, informal spirit of 1896, to the professional, commercial appeal of the 1990s. They have grown enormously; in size from 12 countries and 500 competitors, to a likely 160 countries and 14 000 competitors in Barcelona; in scope, from 9 different sports to 25, each with many more events and disciplines; and in audience, from perhaps half a million to several billion around the world. In scale the Games have developed from a refurbished sixteenth-century stadium (with a misshaped track, and swimming events held in the sea) to the multi-million-pound, purpose-built stadiums without which no budding host city has a chance.

As in any activity, the greatest prizes in sport attract the greatest efforts, the greatest sportsmen and women, and the greatest problems. In human terms, the Games were the first events to attract a terrorist attack (1972), and they were the first to record a death through drugs (1960).

The IOC president has become an international figure, moving around the world like a major head of state. Three

221

very different presidents have overseen the remarkable growth of the last 40 years. The present incumbent, Juan Antonio Samaranch, who continues to be referred to as His Excellency (a title granted him as the Spanish ambassador to Moscow), has held the post since 1980. Lord Killanin, an Irish peer, preceded him for eight years. Before Killanin, one man's reign lasted a full 20 years, and that man was a pivotal and crucial player in the affairs of American athletics and the Olympics in general for 20 years before that. Avery Brundage was a large, bespectacled man from Illinois, USA, the son of a stone-mason, who competed for his country in the 1912 Games before making a fortune in the construction industry. As a self-made American he was proud of his rise from humble origins. Professor Allen Guttman's book *The Games Must Go On* records a tart letter from Brundage to the then IOC Chancellor, Otto Mayer, after a German magazine had criti-cised his 'life of ease'. Brundage wrote: 'you may inform them that every penny I have ever had has been earned through my own efforts.' This was not the only time Brundage was to harp on the theme of self effort.

His first international role was as president of the USOC, and we have already recorded his influence in the debate about the 1936 Games in Berlin. He showed then the stubborn commitment to the Olympic movement that was to become his trademark – as well as what Professor Guttman called his 'inability to imagine sincere opposition'. He was elected the IOC's first vice president in 1946 and became president six years later.

Brundage was an idealist; he passionately believed in sport and in its celebration through the Olympic movement. His favourite quotation was from John Galsworthy: 'Sport, which still keeps the flag of idealism flying, is perhaps the most saving grace in the world at the moment, with its spirit of rules kept, and regard for the adversary, whether the fight is going for or against. When, if ever, the spirit of sport, which is the spirit of fair play, reigns over international affairs, the cat force, which rules there now, will slink away, and human life emerge for the first time from the jungle.' But by 1952, when Brundage took control of the IOC, this was already an old ideal. His overriding belief in amateurism was also an aging one. 'The amateur code,' he wrote, 'coming to us from antiquity, contributed to and strengthened by the noblest aspirations of great men of each generation, embraces the highest moral laws. No philosophy, no religion, preaches loftier sentiments.' He saw the real distinction between amateur and professional as 'a thing of the spirit' which 'exists in the heart and not in the rule book'.

As recently as 1972, at his last Games as president, Brundage sent home the Austrian skier Karl Schranz for appearing in advertisements for a ski manufacturer. He is remembered for manning the Olympic barricades against those he termed 'employees' and 'entertainers'. He once wrote to his old Olympic committee in the USA to query a report that the US Army allowed its Olympians to train full time. He was told that such athletes continued to fulfil their military duties.

Ironically, Brundage probably did as much as anyone to undermine the very thing he held most dear. Alongside the principle of amateurism, Brundage had another essential concern – the universality of the movement itself. But there was a clash between these two great ideals, which began back in the USSR.

When newly established, the Soviet Union had withdrawn from 'bourgeois sport' and thus had never competed in the Games. But following lengthy negotiations after the Second World War, the Russians were elected to the IOC at the 1951 Vienna Congress. For Charles Palmer this was 'the thin end of a very long wedge. It brought in the "state athlete". The Corinthian era was over'.

Brundage can certainly be accused of double standards. He continued throughout his presidency to harass and question those who strayed from his 'true' perception of the amateur ethic. But he must have known that throughout Eastern Europe a façade was erected behind which professional Olympians masqueraded as agricultural or medical students, policemen or soldiers and so on. Brundage was challenged on the point many times and he did indeed press the USSR IOC members for answers about what he himself called 'State amateurism' in a 1954 article. But he felt he had to accept their denials. Professor Guttman says Brundage was much criticised in America as 'a naively imperceptive Communist dupe'.

Charles Palmer recalls suggesting the setting up of 'flying squads' to check whether the members of Russian teams were full-time athletes or not. Brundage's response was that 'they would not get visas.' His own defence was that 'there are probably abuses in the USSR, but there are also abuses in the USA and European countries.' He believed that in the end leaders resolved the problems it was in their power to resolve; and the principle of universality took precedence over the creed of amateurism.

The 'state amateur' creed persisted long after the Brundage era. We talked to Vladimir Pilguy, goalkeeper for Moscow Dynamo, the famous State backed club (originally for the KGB), which claimed to be amateur and which developed so many Olympians (at soccer, gymnastics etc). Pilguy, himself an Olympian in 1972 and 1980, told us: 'We used to say, yes, we are amateurs, students or servicemen, but of course we were in fact professionals ... (sport) was our living.'

But one event alone overshadowed all others in Brundage's reign, and it occurred at his very last Olympics. For over half a century the name of the city of Munich had equalled appeasement; in 1972 it also became synonymous with terrorism. Before dawn on the 5 September, eight Palestinian terrorists invaded the Olympic Village and captured nine Israeli hostages. They demanded the release of 234 prisoners in Israel and freedom for the German terrorists, Andreas Baader and Ulrike Meinhof. After four hours, when some were still wondering how serious an incident this was, the terrorists threw the mutilated body of one of their captives, Moshe Weinberg, into the street. Brundage went to the scene and suggested that the German police use Chicago-style methods. Later that

This picture of a hooded terrorist in the Munich Olympic Village flashed around a horrified world on 5 September 1972. The entire Israeli team were murdered in the incident, and eight terrorists were killed

day, he was criticised by his committee and especially by his successor, Lord Killanin, for getting involved and for failing to convene a meeting of the Executive Board. They felt the matter should have been left to the German authorities and to the German Organising Committee.

Worse was to come. The entire Israeli contingent were to die as well as four of their captors. The words 'Black September' entered the language as the name of a terror group which is still active today.

In spite of a tactless reference to Rhodesia, Brundage's words at the memorial service in a packed stadium the following day were to sum up almost everyone's feelings: 'The Olympic flag and the flags of the world fly at half mast. Sadly, in this imperfect world, the greater and more important the Olympic Games become, the more they are open to commercial, political and now criminal pressure ... We have only the strength of a great ideal ... The Games must go on and we must continue our efforts to keep them clean, pure and honest and try to extend the sportsmanship of the athletic field into other areas.' After 60 years in the movement – as athlete,

225

administrator, spokesman and president – Brundage saw no other option except for the Games to go on. This brought some criticism around the world, but not from within the IOC. He had spoken for them, in his last hour as leader. The Games had to be universal and continuous; they must go on.

But if Brundage and other members, including the newly appointed president, knew how these principles were yet to be tested, they might well have been despondent. The twin pressures of politics and commerce were to grow ever stronger. The issue of South Africa, which had come to the fore under Brundage, brought a boycott of the next Games in Montreal in 1976, triggered by the IOC's refusal to expel the New Zealanders for playing a series of rugby Test matches against South Africa. In 1980, the Americans boycotted Moscow because of Afghanistan. Governments' and politicians' interest in the Games matched the increasing importance of the movement. The rising waters of commercialism, held back to a degree by Brundage playing Canute, rose steadily to a flood.

The progress of the Games in recent years has taken a very different path under President Samaranch. His creed is to meet commercial and political pressures head on and to turn them to the benefit and further growth of Olympism. As a former diplomat, Samaranch has welcomed and often invited the interest of politicians. As an Olympian, and one who sought its further growth in scale and influence, he has embraced the commercial creed. Under his direction the Games themselves have embraced professionalism, in spite of the fact that still no one is paid for actually competing.

Why are the Games so important? Unquestionably, they are the colossus of modern sport. Bestriding the globe, they are at the apex of a glittering pyramid of physical and mental effort, of sporting ambition, of business activity, of media attention and hype and of political debate, negotiation and posturing. The games are a spectacle, a costly, practical reality and a massive administrative task; a dream, representing history and tradition. They represent the power of sport,

226

lasting longer than politicians who sought to use them, and they have adapted and grown from the experience.

They are sport's claim to grace. They are the bloodlines, that generate the continuing quality of today's and tomorrow's actors on the stage of sport. The Olympic Games are sport's link with the ancients – even perhaps with the Gods.

One of the official posters for the Barcelona Games of 1992

227

13 Games for all seasons

Sport is a nonsense, after all; a serious nonsense of course
CLIFF MORGAN, WELSH RUGBY INTERNATIONAL
AND FORMER HEAD OF BBC OUTSIDE BROADCASTS

It's Christmas, 1916, on the Somme. A day of light rain but with some clear periods; a day when sweet memory overcame bitter reality, in the darkness of an interminable conflict. There was no turkey, no crackers, only bully beef as usual. But that Christmas Day soldiers from both sides did something remarkable, in the history of war or sport. They climbed up out of their respective trenches and moved forward, without weapons, and joined to celebrate the day and exchange greetings through the peaceful language of sport. They played soccer in no man's land. No man kept score, but perhaps their Maker did.

Sport has ever been drama's first cousin. The two share village halls and community centres all round the world. Both are an integral part of local life, everywhere. In Britain there are 17 000 societies for amateur drama, with three million members; there are some 125 000 voluntary clubs for the various sports with around six million members. They unite in enthusiasm, in creation, in the fun of collective effort, in helping the community and in helping themselves.

Sport is drama without the script, and it often shows humanity at its finest. In 1964, Anthony Nash and Robin Dixon were representing Britain in the bobsleigh in the

Regal racer. The Princess of Wales comes fourth in the Mothers' Race at the annual Sports Day at Prince Harry's school in south-west London

combined World and Olympic championships at Iglis, in Austria. On the first of their four runs, they clocked the second fastest time, but broke an axle, making withdrawal inevitable. The Italian Eugenio Monti, a great champion of the sport (he won 11 world titles) removed his own axle after his second run and transferred it to the British pair's bob. The next day Nash and Dixon won the gold medal.

Such fair play is the very essence of sport, and such stories are not unique. The best golfers in Britain and America compete every two years for the Ryder Cup, one of sports' most coveted trophies. In 1969, the fate of the match depended upon a duel between the two captains, Tony Jacklin and Jack Nicklaus, and as in the best dramas, they were level on the last green. They would halve and share the cup if Jacklin sank a 3-foot putt, and in those circumstances, no putt is easy. But Nicklaus did not leave anything to chance. In a gesture as grand as any in sport, Nicklaus gave Jacklin the putt. 'I think you'd have got that, don't you?' he said, and the two men shook hands.

Inevitably, every good story is matched by a bad one. In the athletics World Championships in 1987, the Roman hosts were aware of fervent hopes for local heroes and they went too far. In the long jump the Italian Giovanni Evangelisti came fourth, but his distance was 'inflated' to the bronze medal position. The subsequent enquiry by CONI (the Italian Olympic Committee) found there was cheating, but could only condemn junior officials of the Championships. Primo Nebiolo was President of the Italian Federation and also of the Organising Committee of the Championships. Amid public criticism he declined to resign. Subsequently, he was voted out of the presidency of the Italian Federation. He remains as President of the IAAF, one of the most powerful positions in world sport.

In 1919 the Chicago White Sox were playing for the World Series in baseball. The players had a grievance about their small salaries compared to the fortunes made by the owners, and they 'threw' the game in a deal with gambling interests.

Golf's Ryder Cup, 1969, between the USA and Great Britain – a draw, settled with a sportsman's handshake between Jack Nicklaus of America (left) and Tony Jacklin of Britain.

230

Outside the stadium after the game, a group of boys encountered one of the great White Sox stars of the day, 'Shoeless Joe' Jackson, outside the Chicago ground. 'Say it ain't so, Joe' one of them said. The small boys know how sport should be – and we should not let them down.

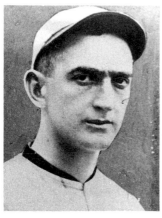

'Say it ain't so, Joe', the small boys asked for everyone, but 'Shoeless Joe' Jackson could not answer. The World Series in Chicago had been fixed. It was more than a game

Today, sport is big numbers, big business, big news, big money, big media messages and a force the world's politicians cannot ignore.

But what is its truth? After all what we see most clearly today is its contradictions. Sport is equal, for example – its basis is free and fair competition – but it has always been mixed with prejudice. Governing bodies, national and international, profess the principle of equality. They echo Sir Winston Churchill, who said: 'In sport, in courage, and in the sight of Heaven, all men meet on equal terms.' But they don't do enough to allow everyone to compete equally; national pride often prevents a rigorous clampdown on drugs, for instance. And women are not treated equally. Many blacks, coloureds and Jews still worry about the whisper if not the lash of racism. Christians, like the English triple-jumper Jonathan Edwards, do not want to compete on a Sunday, but find that this excludes them from major competitions.

Sport is open to all; but some clubs are closed, facilities and equipment remain beyond the reach of many. Competition is open if you have the right connections – and they may mean your agent. Sport is free, but it can be costly. Sport is healthy, but you can get injured and perhaps die. Before you do, the hard regimen of training and competition could lead to arthritis and other unwanted ailments in later life. Sport is independent, but it depends on sponsors, promoters, supporters and often governments. It has mortgaged its house and, some fear, its soul.

Sport is full of contradictions – it has a crisis of identity. So what are its 'real' achievements?

'Sport is the most unifying influence in the world today,' according to Sir Dennis Follows, then Chairman of the BOA, and he said it at the height of the row over the Moscow Olympics. And we can all see it, in events like the London Marathon and its lookalikes around the world, where sportsmen and sportswomen give rather than take. They take part, rather than compete. They are not seekers after the 'faster, higher, stronger' creed of the Olympic movement. They are, for the most part, amateurs, they even pay their own expenses. They are their own coach, driver, promoter and sponsor. The Arab promoter of cricket's Asia Cup, Abdul Rahman Bukhatir, recognised this basic need; 'Sport,' he said, 'is a means of providing pleasure to people – it is like offering clothes to those who need them.'

Every Sunday morning in Britain about one million people play soccer. They play usually in local leagues, organised and run under the auspices of the Football Association, but they are one million miles away from the stadiums and skills of the England team the FA also runs. These amateurs play on pitches provided and maintained by local councils, where the bounce is at best uneven, the lines may not always be precise or even clear, and where the changing rooms and the lavatories are sometimes in the nearest trees.

One of the authors of this book runs such a team in his village of Oxshott in Surrey, not far from London. Every Sunday morning David Teasdale is chairman and coach, and he carries the kit. At home games he often has to referee as well, because he will be the only one there who is qualified. Sometimes, he is also substitute, but then his wife worries about his health! His team of boys has just started in men's football. They are learning a new form of the game and also a new language; at this level, both can be crude.

Around the world, sport is evenings and weekends, the occasional day off or holiday, families and friends. It is sweating, showering and singing together, drinking and eating together, packing up and going home together, it is winning and losing together. Sport is part of the social round, from Oxshott to Oman, from village to metropolis, from nation to nation. People play sport to meet people, to share a fun experience, to pass the time, to climb a local ladder, social or sporting; to feel better, because they enjoy it or because they believe it is good for them. Sport is conclusively more than a game, whatever its roots.

Nick Faldo was inspired to take up golf after watching, enthralled, as Jack Nicklaus showed how easy and beautiful a game it was. Top performers can make it all look so simple. They strip any sport down to its bare, technical essentials, making us all feel we could do it ourselves. Let's listen to the commentator: 'Steffi Graf serves wide to her opponent's backhand, it's fast, she stretches, just reaches the ball, returns it just over the net, Graf volleys to the right hand corner, 15-love, just too good ...' There was nothing her opponent could do. The serve and the volley were expertly placed. And it all looked so easy.

Germany's Steffi Graf makes the game look so easy

234

Sport at the top is now a career, but a special career, because sport is a special business. Neither can depend wholly on the normal rules of the market. Sport has to remain sport, a concept rooted in the track and not on the balance sheet. It has to be true to its principles, rather than its traditions, even though some are the same. But the major principle, and the greatest tradition of sport, is fair play, which at its simplest means no cheating – doing nothing against the rules, or the spirit of the rules. It is that which makes sport unique, and it makes winning no less important. Sportsmen and women can win fairly. There is no contradiction between fair play and results. Indeed, it is their conjunction that is the essence of sport and its unique contribution to society. And it is the first responsibility of all of us, but particularly leaders, managers and coaches, to resolve the conflict between the game and the result. Then the words of the American sports writer, Grantland Rice, who died in 1954, would not seem so out of date: '*For when the great scorer comes to write against your name, He marks not how you won or lost, but how you played the game*'.

All round the world, in all weathers, millions enjoy sport. Thousands enjoy the annual ski marathon in Switzerland

235

Bibliography

ALLSPORT   *Visions of sport* Pelham, 1988. op.

AMOS, H. and LANG, A.   *These were the Greeks* Thames & Hudson, 1989; pb, 1991

ARIS, S.   *Sportsbiz: inside the sports business* Hutchinson, 1990

BARNETT, S.   *Games and sets: the changing face of sport and television* BFI, 1990

CANTER, D. et al.   *Football in its place* Routledge, 1989

CASHMORE, E.   *Making sense of sport* Routledge, 1990

COE, S. and MASON, N.   *The Olympians* Pavilion, 1988

COE, S. and P.   *Running for fitness* Pavilion, 1988

COOTE, J.   *History of the Olympics in pictures* Tom Stacey, 1972. op.

ESPY, R.   *The politics of the Olympic games* University of California Press, 1979; pb, 1981

EVANS, H. ed.   *Front page history* Quiller Press, 1984

FAWCETT, R. et al.   *Climbing* Bell & Hyman, 1986. op.

FRANCIS, C.   *Speed trap* Grafton, 1991

GREEN, G.   *History of the Football Association* Naldrett Press, 1953. op.

GUTTMAN, A.   *The Games must go on* Columbia UP, 1984

HARGREAVES, J. ed.   *Sport, culture and ideology* Routledge, 1982

HART-DAVIS, D.   *Hitler's Olympics: the 1936 Games* Hodder & Stoughton, new edn, 1988

HEMERY, D.   *The pursuit of sporting excellence* Willow, 1986. op; *Sporting excellence* 2nd edn, Harper Collins, 1991

HEMINGWAY, E.   *Death in the afternoon* Panther, 1977

HICKS, W. ed.   *'News Chronicle' boys' book of all sports* News Chronicle, 1950

HOLT, R.   *Sport and the British: a modern history* OUP, 1989; pb, 1990

JAMES, S. ed.   *Chambers sporting quotations* Chambers, 1990

KIMMAGE, P.   *A rough ride: insight into professional cycling* S. Paul, 1990; pb, 1991

LEWIS, C. and MARX, J.   *Inside track: my professional life in amateur track and field* Pelham, 1990; Sphere, 1991

MATTHEWS, P. and MORRISON, I.   *Encyclopedia of international sports records and results* Guinness, 1990

McINTOSH, P.   *Sport in society* West London Press, 1987. op.

MESSEROLE, M. ed.   *The 1991 information please sports almanac* Houghton Mifflin, 1990

MORRISON, I.   *The Guinness guide to Formula One* Guinness, 1990

MOSS, S.   *Fangio: a Pirelli album* Pavilion, 1991

MOYNIHAN, C. and COE, S.   *The misuse of drugs in sport* Department of the Environment, 1987

Official national football league record and fact book Partridge, 1991

Organisation of sport and recreation in Britain Central Council of Physical Recreation, 1991

PALMER, C.   *The committee of enquiry into amateur status and participation in sport* Central Council of Physical Recreation, 1988

RIORDAN, J. ed.   *Sport under communism* Hurst, 1981

SAMUEL, J. ed.   *Guardian book of sports quotes* Queen Anne Press, 1985. op.

SINGER, B.   *100 Years of the Paris Tribune* Harry N. Abrams Inc., New York, 1987

SMITH, R.   *Sport and freedom: rise of big-time college athletics* NY, OUP, 1989; pb 1991

Sponsorship of sport by tobacco companies in the UK: terms of agreement between the Minister of Sport, Tobacco Advisory Council and Imported Tobacco Products Advisory Council Department of the Environment, 1987

VOY, R. and DEETER, K.   *Drugs, sport and politics* Leisure Press, 1991

WALLECHINSKY, D.   *Complete book of the Olympics* Penguin, 1988. op; Aurum, new edn, Jan 1992

WILLIAMS, J. et al.   *Hooligans abroad: behaviour and control of English fans in continental Europe* Routledge, 1989

WILSON, J.   *Politics and leisure* Unwin Hyman, 1988

WILSON, N.   *The sports business: the men and the money* Piatkus, 1988; Mandarin, 1990

Index